HEADLINE SERIES

No. 297   FOREIGN POLICY ASSOCIATION   Fall 1991

The Soviet Breakup and U.S. Foreign Policy

by Allen Lynch

Cover Design: Ed Bohon $4.00
Photo: AP/Wide World Photos

SO-AGC-754

The Author

ALLEN LYNCH is currently associate professor of government and foreign affairs at the University of Virginia. From July 1989 to May 1992 he was assistant director of the W. Averell Harriman Institute for Advanced Study of the Soviet Union at Columbia University. After receiving a Ph.D. in political science from Columbia University, Dr. Lynch worked at the Institute for East-West Security Studies in New York City for five years. A specialist in Soviet foreign policy and East-West relations, he is the author of many books, as well as numerous articles for leading magazines and newspapers.

❧

I dedicate this book to my mother.

The Foreign Policy Association

The Foreign Policy Association is a private, nonprofit, nonpartisan educational organization. Its purpose is to stimulate wider interest and more effective participation in, and greater understanding of, world affairs among American citizens. Among its activities is the continuous publication, dating from 1935, of the HEADLINE SERIES. The author is responsible for factual accuracy and for the views expressed. FPA itself takes no position on issues of U.S. foreign policy.

HEADLINE SERIES (ISSN 0017-8780) is published four times a year, Winter, Spring, Summer and Fall, by the Foreign Policy Association, Inc., 729 Seventh Ave., New York, N.Y. 10019. Chairman, Michael H. Coles; President, R.T. Curran; Editor in Chief, Nancy L. Hoepli; Senior Editors, Ann R. Monjo and K.M. Rohan. Subscription rates, $15.00 for 4 issues; $25.00 for 8 issues; $30.00 for 12 issues. Single copy price $4.00. Discount 25% on 10 to 99 copies; 30% on 100 to 499; 35% on 500 to 999; 40% on 1,000 or more. Payment must accompany all orders. Postage and handling: $2.50 first copy; $.50 each additional copy. Second-class postage paid at New York, N.Y. POSTMASTER: Send address changes to HEADLINE SERIES, Foreign Policy Association, 729 Seventh Ave., New York, N.Y. 10019. Copyright 1992 by Foreign Policy Association, Inc. Design by K.M. Rohan. Printed at Science Press, Ephrata, Pennsylvania. Fall 1991. Published June 1992.

Library of Congress Catalog Card No. 92-71574
ISBN 0-87124-146-3

The Historic Significance of the Disintegration of the U.S.S.R.

In mid-1947, as the cold war congealed, the U.S. State Department's Soviet expert George F. Kennan wrote that "Soviet society may well contain deficiencies which will eventually weaken its own total potential." Kennan argued that "the United States has it in its power to increase enormously the strains under which Soviet policy must now operate, to force upon the Kremlin a far greater degree of moderation and circumspection than it has had to observe in recent years, and in this way to promote tendencies which must eventually find their outlet in either the breakup or the gradual mellowing of Soviet power." Forty-five years later the world confronted the consequences of the breakup of the U.S.S.R. The Union of Soviet Socialist Republics had been replaced in December 1991 by the Commonwealth of Independent States. The 11 states that constitute the commonwealth have decided to regulate their relationships by international treaty and consultation instead of mutual submission to a federal or even a much looser confederal union. (Georgia is the only former Soviet

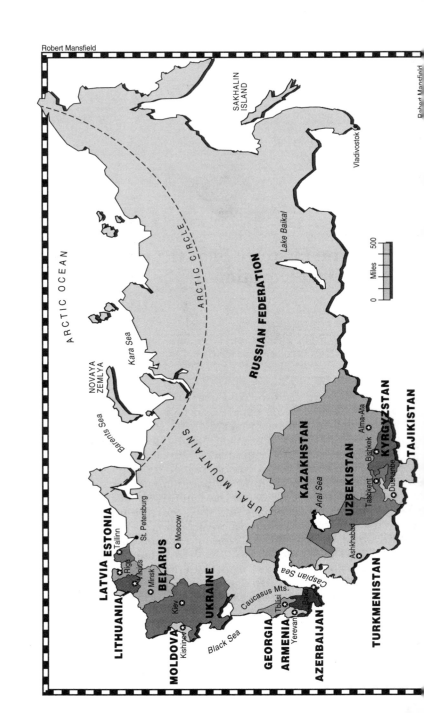

Robert Mansfield

republic, aside from the Baltic states of Estonia, Latvia and Lithuania, that has refused to be part of the commonwealth.)

For the first time in this century (and in some cases, like that of Ukraine, in several centuries), the Russian state must deal with its neighbors in Central Asia, the Caucasus in the mountainous south, and especially in Slavic Belarus (formerly Belorussia) and Ukraine, as equals rather than as colonies. Furthermore, Russia can no longer simply command obedience, even within its own confines, although with three fourths of the landmass and half the population of the former Soviet Union it is the virtual successor to the U.S.S.R.

The beginnings of meaningful constitutional government in Russia, reflected in the popular election of Boris N. Yeltsin as its president in June 1991, have signified the end of absolutist government, whether it be the despotism of one man, as under the czars, or of one party, as under the Communists. Government in Russia is beginning to become accountable to its people. The likelihood that a single state might mobilize the resources of territories encompassing fully one sixth of the world's land surface in a hostile political or military campaign against the outside world has, for the foreseeable future, vanished and with it the overwhelming public justification for the international role the United States has played since 1945 in containing Soviet Communist power.

As a result of this unexpected historic development, the United States and its major allies now find themselves called upon to deal with the consequences of success. Having long ago accustomed themselves to deterring and defeating Soviet political and military offensives, the United States and its allies are suddenly forced to address a host of other problems emanating from the disintegration of the U.S.S.R. Can the former Soviet nuclear arsenal, still numbering over 25,000 weapons, be insulated from an unstable political environment? Can the outside world, especially the countries of East Central Europe, protect themselves against the collapse of trade with their former Soviet partner? Can Western Europe insure itself against the prospect of millions of economic and political refugees escaping possibly intolerable conditions in the former Soviet lands? More particularly, can the international community prevent, or at least contain, post-Soviet territorial disputes from spilling over into the dozen states that border the countries of the former U.S.S.R.? Finally, what is the nature of the international stake in the economic and political reform of Russia and its post-Soviet neighbors, and how can the outside world best promote their chances for success?

Challenge to the New World Order

The collapse of the U.S.S.R. has, curiously, challenged the hopeful American vision of a "new world order." That order, as Soviet-American diplomacy during the 1990–91 embargo and war against Iraq showed, depended upon a stable as well as a cooperative Soviet counterpart. Indeed, the prospects for a constructive future world order will be determined in large measure by how questions concerning the transformation of the U.S.S.R. are addressed.

It is difficult to overstate the significance of the collapse of the Soviet state, which took place in 1990–91. Within the span of 12 months (December 1990 to December 1991), the Soviet political system passed through the following phases:

- **December 1990:** Soviet President Mikhail S. Gorbachev's abandonment of his alliance with the radical democrats, which led to the resignation of foreign minister Eduard A. Shevardnadze and the abortive military crackdown in the Baltic states in January 1991;

- **March–April 1991:** Gorbachev's realignment with the forces advocating sovereignty for the republics, as shown by an April 23 agreement with Yeltsin and leaders of eight other republics granting them "an essential increase" in their role in decisionmaking in exchange for cooperation with Gorbachev's union government in maintaining public order;

- **June 1991:** The election of Yeltsin as Russian president in a free, competitive, popular election, the first such mandate in over a millennium of Russian history;

- **July 1991:** Further indications of the virtual crumbling of Soviet power, as Gorbachev concedes to the republics exclusive power of taxation, with only a small percentage to be forwarded to the union government; separately, the conclusion of a bilateral, Russian-Lithuanian treaty recognizing Lithuanian independence in exchange for Lithuanian guarantees of the civil rights of Russians living in the republic;

- **August–September 1991:** The reaction of the old guard to the collapse of the Soviet system as elements of the Communist party and military leadership stage an anti-Gorbachev coup to preserve the union government and fail; the emergence of Yeltsin as the dominant leader in the country, eclipsing Gorbachev, who is still trying to preserve the union and initially even the Communist party as an agent of reform. On August 29, Russia and Ukraine sign a treaty whose preamble refers to "the former U.S.S.R.," thereby exposing what was becoming a reality.

• **November 1991:** The formal bankruptcy of the Soviet state, as its treasury, deprived of a tax base, concedes that it is unable to pay for the functions of government; the burden is rapidly assumed by Yeltsin's Russian government;

• **December 1991:** On December 8, in effect a second anti-Gorbachev coup: the sudden signature by Russia, Ukraine and Belarus in Minsk, the Belarusian capital, of an agreement to found the Commonwealth of Independent States, replacing the U.S.S.R. and rendering Gorbachev, as Soviet president, irrelevant. Within a fortnight, nearly all of the former Soviet republics sign on (with amendments) to the commonwealth in Alma-Ata, the Kazakhstan capital. On December 25, Gorbachev, bowing to the inevitable, resigns as the last president of the Soviet Union;

• **January 1992:** Radical market reforms, including the comprehensive abolition of price controls, begin in early January in Russia and the other republics.

Gorbachev's Reforms

In historical perspective, the course of reform throughout the Gorbachev years (1985–91) represents a break with the classical pattern of reforms in Russia. Historically, the state initiated reforms to improve its international competitiveness but would suspend them in mid-course for fear of ceding too much power to society and to the non-Russians within the empire. Even liberal Russians hesitated to undermine an autocracy which, in the czarist period as well as in Soviet times, provided for the dominance of the Russian ruling class over the non-Russian (as well as Russian) parts of the empire and assured the country's great-power status abroad. This is the insight captured by the nineteenth century Russian poet Mikhail Lermontov, who in describing Russia's historic dominance of an entire continent and more than 100 peoples wrote, "We may be slaves, but enslaved by Russia, the Ruler of the Universe."

Gorbachev, who sought to introduce a socialist version of constitutional government to the Soviet Union, proved willing to court risks that made his predecessors flinch. In the process, he actually justified the hesitations of those earlier leaders because his reforms unleashed forces which destroyed the empire at home and rolled back its power abroad. Yet, in the end, it may be that only the forces of nationalism that overtook Gorbachev's reforms were capable of introducing the kind of constitutional government that was also the aim of his complex agenda of economic and political reform. What is perhaps most striking about the Gorbachev years is the relative absence of mass, politically motivated violence. Certainly, there has been intense internecine warfare among national groups and political factions in the Caucasus region, in the republics of Georgia, Armenia and Azerbaijan. But to date, for better or worse, this has been violence of a local character, with little prospect of spreading to the broader regions of the former U.S.S.R. (In early 1992, Turkey, Iran and the Conference on Security and Cooperation in Europe, or CSCE, Europe's leading political and human-rights forum to which the United States and Canada belong, were each involved in various attempts to negotiate an Armenian-Azerbaijani cease-fire; in Moldova—formerly called Moldavia—a siege had set in between the Slavic inhabitants of eastern Moldova and the ethnically Romanian Moldovan state, involving elements of the ex-Soviet 14th Army.) About 2,000 people are thought to have been killed in politically related violence during the six Gorbachev years. For all of the human tragedy that this entails, in light of the unprecedented scope of social change in the Gorbachev era, this is a remarkably low figure.

Consider that there has been a fourfold set of transformations buffeting Soviet, and now post-Soviet society: in the economy, the political system, the nature of relations between the nations making up the U.S.S.R., and in foreign policy. In brief, the Soviet economy has been dismantled from above and has yet to be effectively replaced by the market system that is the declared aim of the Russian reformers. In political terms, Gorbachev destroyed the remnants of the institutional and psychological order—centralization and fear, respectively—created by Joseph Stalin's dictatorship (1924–53) but was unable to set in place an alternative political system. The collapse of the Soviet state signalled the end of direct Russian political control over the non-Russian nations of the empire.

Reuters/Bettmann

Moscow, August 19, 1991: Russian Federation President Boris N. Yeltsin, standing on a tank in front of the Russian parliament, vows to fight the coup that overthrew the Gorbachev government.

Finally, in foreign policy, as early as 1989 Gorbachev's tolerance encouraged the East European satellites of the U.S.S.R. to recapture their independence and expel the Soviet Union, politically and militarily, from their countries, in the process undermining its claim to the status of a global political power. Indeed, it may be argued that Russia, as the de facto successor-state to the U.S.S.R., is not a superpower but simply an important state in the international political system: Russia still counts by dint of its sheer mass— its land, people and resources— yet economically it is not even in the same league with the lesser European economies, not to mention Germany or Japan.

Any one of these changes happening alone would qualify as a major revolution in its own right. That all four are taking place in the most essential spheres of political and economic life, and without generalized political violence, is remarkable when compared to any of the other great revolutions of the past two centuries. In important respects, political scientists and economists do not have the theoretical tools to understand the breadth and pace of transformations that have been shaking the Soviet and post-Soviet landscape. For example, no one has ever witnessed the invention of a market economy from the ground up. Markets, like most social institutions, have evolved organically over centuries. Likewise, very few if any "loose" confederations have witnessed the sort of dynamic international diplomacy by their constituent political units that characterized the conduct of the Soviet Union's republics in 1990 and 1991. Even the American Articles of Confederation, criticized for giving too much power to the states, explicitly prohibited them from engaging in independent diplomacy, with foreign states or among themselves.

Understanding the Soviet Transformation

If scholars in their leisured reflections confront basic difficulties in coming to terms with change in Russia and the other lands of the former Soviet Union, it should not be surprising to find that harried government officials in the West, including the United States, have had enormous difficulty just understanding the fact of Soviet disintegration, not to mention its manifold consequences. Throughout 1990 and 1991 the United States and its European allies made repeated efforts to sustain a central Soviet government that had already outlived its time. The United States made it clear from the onset of the Lithuanian sovereignty crisis in March 1990 that it would not permit its formal obligations regarding Baltic independence to interfere with its broader Soviet policy, which was focused on the person and policies of President Gorbachev. Gorbachev, and by implication the United States, was dedicated to reforming the union, not to triggering its disintegration, however peaceful. President George Bush even ventured to Kiev, capital of non-Russian Ukraine, in August 1991 and inveighed against what he termed suicidal nationalism. Such undertakings may even have convinced some in the Communist party and military leadership that the West valued the preservation of the union over the democratizing tendencies that were sure to dissolve it. Statements by coup leader Gennadi Yanayev on August 19, 1991, the first day of the coup, about the need to preserve "stability" in a "nuclear superpower" (an expressed Western interest), as well as the junta's stated desire to respect existing international agreements reached with the West, lend credence to this view. Having concluded that Gorbachev's reforms were no longer consistent with the preserva-

Muscovites celebrating the defeat of the coup of August 1991.

tion of that union, some of those plotting the August 1991 coup may have convinced themselves that their efforts to preserve a union whose integrity the West had for some time been seeking to maintain would find acquiescence in the West. That they were mistaken, and that the West erroneously sent the wrong signal, underscores the difficulty in communicating clearly between different political cultures. It also reflects the particular difficulty that the United States has had in relating to the U.S.S.R. as anything other than "the other superpower."

There are, in fact, at least three reasons why the United States has found it difficult to react effectively to the dissolution of the U.S.S.R. First, the U.S.S.R. had been part of the pattern of East-West relations for decades. Over that time the United States and its allies had found ways of accommodating themselves to the reality of Soviet power. This took two forms: agreeing to live with a divided Germany within a divided Europe as the least harmful outcome of World War II; and learning to live with nuclear weapons and the restraints that they imposed on U.S.-Soviet relations. Nuclear-arms control became the most visible symbol of this limited understanding between the two superpowers. Second, the United States—its people, its government, and even many of its academics—have been unable to relate to the U.S.S.R. as a distinct kind of multinational state. Differences among the nationalities of the U.S.S.R. were usually seen as regional, or even folkloric, and seldom as central to the definition of the individual's relationship to state and society, and hence to the governability of the unitary Soviet party-state. Third, Western policy in general, and U.S. policy in particular, became in the late 1980s very closely identified with Gorbachev's vision of the Soviet future, and thus with his definition of the permissible limits of change in the country. Since the very essence of Gorbachev's reform was to adapt the union system to contemporary international conditions, the West's view of its own interests in Soviet policies tended to reflect Gorbachev's views as to the relative unimportance of nationalism in the U.S.S.R.

Indeed, the key to understanding the fate of reform in Gorbachev's U.S.S.R., and the future of American interests in the post-Soviet world, lies in coming to terms with the character and tendencies of nationalism in Russia, Ukraine, and the other republics of the former U.S.S.R. The significance of nationalism can hardly be exaggerated. In December 1991, U.S. Secretary of State James A. Baker 3d stated his concern that the Soviet Union might become a kind of Yugoslavia with nuclear weapons, rent by civil strife in an unprecedentedly dangerous nuclear environment. However remote such an outcome might be, the possibility itself warrants careful study of the problem for two reasons. First, the U.S.S.R. did resemble Yugoslavia as a nominally federal (though in practice heavily centralist) Communist-party state, one that was multinational in composition, with ethnically based political-territorial units ("republics") as its constituent parts. Second, neither the government nor American academics have given serious thought to the prospect that a major nuclear power might also become an unstable state. What, for instance, does this imply for the U.S. approach to nuclear deterrence and nuclear-arms control? And equally important, what does the collapse of the U.S.S.R., which has been the major justification for American global policy and commitments since 1945, signify for the ways in which the United States defines its international interests, the means it chooses to advance those interests, and, relatedly, the allocation of human and material resources at home?

The Multinational U.S.S.R.:
Facts and Figures

Most Americans are aware that the territories that the U.S.S.R. encompassed are vast by any comparison, covering one sixth of the world's land surface and 11 time zones. The U.S.S.R. as a whole occupied a territory about as large as that of the United States and Canada combined. Russia constitutes the overwhelming bulk of the U.S.S.R.'s patrimony, with about three fourths of the landmass of the U.S.S.R. and a comparable proportion of its natural and economic resources. Yet, ethnic Russians, who total 147 million (compared to approximately 250 million Americans in 1990), accounted for barely half the population of the former U.S.S.R. (just under 290 million, according to the 1989 census). The other half of the former Soviet population is distributed among dozens of nations, including 14 that before 1991 possessed their own ethnically based republics within the union. These range from Ukraine, comparable to France in size and population (52 million people), to the three Baltic states, whose ethnic Baltic populations combined totaled some 5 million, to the 50 million mainly Turkic Muslim population of Soviet Central Asia. Each of these republics possessed its own official native language, which contested with Russian as lingua franca within republican borders, and, according to the Soviet constitution, possessed the right to secede from the U.S.S.R. (Neither the constitution nor the legal code until 1990 spelled out how the republics were to exercise that right.)

These few facts highlight a reality that has historically been far from apparent to Americans, whether in or out of government: the U.S.S.R. was indeed a multinational state. Beneath the surface of unity imposed by the Communist party of the Soviet Union, the country's effective governing agent, the distinctions between the nations that made up the U.S.S.R. are more comparable to those between the nations of Europe than to those between the American states, a comparison that Americans frequently and mistakenly make. In fact, problems associated with ethnic and national relations are often more complex in the territories of the former Soviet Union than in Europe. Unlike in Western Europe, where the nation-state has generally become deeply established, the peoples of the Soviet Union are characterized by extensive interpenetration, with millions of people living outside of their ethnic homelands, as well as widespread intermarriage among the three major Slavic populations of the country (Russians, Ukrainians, and Belarusians).

By way of example, 25 million Russians live outside of Russia proper, in eastern and southern Ukraine, northern Kazakhstan and Belarus, in addition to locally large percentages in the two Baltic states of Latvia and Estonia. All of these regions border on Russian territory. Significant Russian populations are also found in Uzbekistan and Kyrgyzstan. The possibility that national tensions might combine with territorial claims to incite civil strife (as has happened between Armenia and Azerbaijan, and within Georgia and Moldova) is implicit in such a political and demographic profile and cannot be ignored. Indeed, it is precisely such a dynamic that lies behind the war that Serbia, the largest republic in Yugoslavia, unleashed on Croatia in June 1991, following the Croatian declaration of independence. (About 500,000 Serbs live within Croatian borders and make up about 10 percent of Croatia's population.) Conversely, another 35 million people from the non-Russian republics of the Soviet Union live outside their ethnic homelands, the largest segment in Russia, but in fact distributed throughout the former Soviet territories. Thus, out of a total population of some 290 million, over 60 million, or more than 20 percent, live beyond the frontiers of their national homelands.

Ethnic Fears Spur Baltics' Drive for Independence

If this framework is applied to the Baltic states, for example, it is clear why ethnic Balts' alarm about the immigration of Russians and Ukrainians played a catalytic role in their drive for independence in 1988 and 1989. Naturally, the Baltic peoples—Estonians, Latvians, and Lithuanians—had never given up their dream of recovering the independence lost in 1940 when Stalin's U.S.S.R. annexed the three states consequent to the secret provisions of the Nazi-Soviet Non-Aggression Pact of August 1939. (The pact guaranteed German Führer Adolf Hitler Soviet cooperation in invading Poland, thus triggering World War II.) Between 1940 and 1941 and again between 1945 and 1949, 200,000 Baltic citizens were deported to Siberia, where many of them perished. Yet it was the greater political openness afforded by the Gorbachev reforms that emboldened them to act. For the Balts, that openness was most dramatically expressed by Moscow's establishment of an official government commission to review—and in the end to reject—the legality of the secret Nazi-Soviet agreement. A key issue, especially for the Latvians and Estonians, was the high and increasing percentage of non-Baltic populations, mainly Russians and Ukrainians, in their countries. Indeed, Latvians, who make up just over 50 percent of the total population of Latvia and constitute a distinct minority in the Latvian capital of Riga, were on the verge of becoming a minority in their own country. The same tendency was observable in Estonia, where ethnic Estonians make up about 65 percent of the population. Russians and Ukrainians, mainly immigrants brought in by the Soviet government after 1945 to industrialize the region and buttress Soviet rule there, make up 40 percent of the Latvian population and nearly a third of the Estonian.

Baltic concerns were not without justification. In the republic of Kazakhstan, literally the land of the Kazakhs, the Kazakh people had in the course of the Soviet period been reduced to about 36 percent of the population of their own country. Russians and Ukrainians, brought there since the 1930s to populate new industrial regions and settle vast agricultural lands in the north, make up 41 percent and 6 percent, respectively, of the population of Kazakhstan, thus constituting a Slavic plurality (or, including the 5 percent German population, a virtual European majority). With such a prospect facing the Latvians and Estonians, who—unlike the Kazakhs—judged their economic prospects better served apart from the union, the Baltic peoples exploited the opportunity of *glasnost* (openness) and began their remarkable campaign for independence.

A more detailed analysis of the population statistics adds sharp focus to the multinational dynamics of what for want of a better term will be called the Soviet populations. Whereas the Slavs and the Balts are reproducing well below the replacement rate (far less than two children per family), the 50 million Muslims of Central Asia, who made up about 18 percent of the former Soviet Union population and were the equivalent of 35 percent of the Russian population, average five to six children per family and are doubling in population every 20 years. At this rate, before the second quarter of the next century, the number of Muslims in Central Asia should exceed half of the total Russian population of the former U.S.S.R. Whether the Russians will want to maintain any close political association with a Central Asia that is on its way to achieving population parity with Russia is an open question. The point for purposes of analysis is that the national differences between, say, the Baltic republic of Estonia and the Central Asian republic of Uzbekistan are as great as those between Canada and Saudi Arabia. America's fixation on the U.S.S.R. as the other superpower has distorted its understanding of the very complex nationality issues that always lay under the surface of apparent Soviet political stability and which have now risen to dominate the politics of the post-Soviet era.

A Review of the Soviet Peoples

The following review is necessarily schematic, as it cannot hope to cover all of the hundreds of different ethnic and linguistic groups that made up the U.S.S.R. Since the post-Soviet political landscape is dominated by the efforts of leaders of the former U.S.S.R.'s republics to define a nationalist political and economic agenda for their people, coverage is limited to them. The Baltic states of Estonia, Latvia and Lithuania have expressed no desire to become associated politically with the new Commonwealth of

Independent States. They are therefore not covered here. Of the remaining 12 republics, Georgia alone did not accede to the commonwealth agreement upon signature. The 11 remaining republics may be classified primarily as Slavs (Russia, Ukraine and Belarus) and Muslims (Kazakhstan, Azerbaijan, Kyrgyzstan, Tajikistan, Turkmenistan and Uzbekistan), and include the Christian Armenians and Moldovans, the latter actually being mostly ethnic Romanians. In spite of the determination of each of these republics, now in effect nation-states, to pursue independent foreign and domestic policies, they will find it difficult to do so given their high degree of economic dependence on each other. The system of centralized Soviet economic planning treated the economies of the different republics of the U.S.S.R. as a single whole. As the former Soviet republics establish their political independence, they are discovering that they remain closely bound by the legacy of Soviet central planning.

The economies of all of the republics save Russia are heavily dependent on trade with the other republics for their economic stability. Of the non-Russian areas, Ukraine has the lowest degree of such dependency: somewhat more than 30 percent of its economy depends on trade with the other republics (mainly Russia). For all of the others (including the Baltic states), economic dependency on the former Soviet republics—again, mainly Russia—ranges from 40 percent to over 60 percent. By contrast, the Russian economy—due to the size of its domestic market—is only about 17 percent dependent on trade with the other republics. None of the successor-states to the Soviet Union can hope to survive economically without a smooth economic, and thus political, relationship with Russia.

I. The Slavs: Russia, Ukraine and Belarus
Russian Federation

While ethnic Russians constitute about 82 percent of Russia's total population, the Russian state, like the Soviet state before it, is a federation. The Russian Federation contains 38 official national minorities, many endowed with varying degrees of political and administrative autonomy. These "autonomous" regions occupy about 27 percent of the territory of the Russian Federation. (This percentage doubles to 54 percent if all other areas defined by ethnicity, such as the Chukchi district, are taken into account.) Almost all of the hundreds of nations and ethnic groups that made up the Soviet Union are found represented on Russian territory. These peoples range from the Eskimo-related Chukchi and Yakuts in far eastern Siberia (Yakutia, twice the size of Alaska, is the repository of most Russian gold and diamond mines), to Tatars, Jews, Ossetians (split with Georgia), and the Muslim Chechen and Ingush peoples bordering the southern Caucasus region. (In November 1991 the Chechen-Ingush autonomous region declared its independence from Russia, provoking the dispatch of troops by Yeltsin. Yeltsin quickly rescinded his act in the face of opposition by the Russian parliament.)

Furthermore, as noted earlier, about 25 million Russians live outside of Russia, including over 11 million in Ukraine, over 6 million in Kazakhstan, almost 2 million in Uzbekistan, 1.3 million in Belarus, and more than 1.5 million in the three Baltic states. With more than three fourths of the territory of the former U.S.S.R., Russia has about 51 percent of the former Soviet population and accounted for 61 percent of its total economic output. Russia is the world's largest producer of oil and natural gas, and has by far the world's largest proven reserves of natural gas.

The historic Russian state was actually founded by a Viking people called the Varangians, or Rus, who established a state based in Kiev (A.D. 882–1169), capital of present-day Ukraine, to guarantee their trade between the Baltic and the Byzantine Empire. Kievan Russia reached the apex of its geographic rule by 1054, whereupon control in succeeding centuries shifted between various Slavic princes under pressure from Germanic tribes in the west and the conquest by the Mongol horde to the east. In the course of the late Middle Ages, the focus of Russian power shifted from Kiev to Novgorod in the north and eventually to Moscow, where in the mid-sixteenth century Czar Ivan IV ("the Terrible") secured his domination over the Russian heartland and began a drive eastward which extended to the Ural mountains (1600) and the Pacific Ocean (1725). Throughout this period, and up until the Russian Revolution of 1917, the Russian political system was an autocracy, that is, there was one absolute ruler, the czar, and the country was his effective patrimony. (A weak parliament, the Duma, was introduced following defeat by Japan in the war of 1904–5.) The Communist revolution in 1917 in essence adapted the autocratic principle to rule by one party, the Communist party, and through military superiority, political organization and sheer terror established the Union of Soviet Socialist Republics as the successor-state to the Russian Empire. It was the Russian people who suffered the bulk of the more than 28 million deaths and a comparable number of wounded inflicted by the Nazis during World War II, as well as the bulk of the tens of millions of peacetime casualties inflicted by the Communists, mainly during the rule of Vladmir I. Lenin (1917–24) and Stalin.

After the decline and, in 1991, collapse of the U.S.S.R., the Russian Federation, ruled by the popularly elected President Yeltsin, took over the institutions of Soviet power while agreeing to live with the non-Russian former Soviet republics as a coequal sovereign state. It is in this capacity that Russia and the other republics have agreed to participate in the Commonwealth of Independent States. The accords were signed in Minsk and Alma-Ata in December 1991. For the foreseeable future, the main business of the commonwealth will center around negotiations over the redistribution of Soviet assets, including the military, between Russia and its former Soviet neighbors.

Ukraine

Ukraine is the second richest and second-most populous republic of the former U.S.S.R. Of its 52 million people, almost 40 million are ethnic Ukrainians; about 11 million are Russian; slightly over half a million are Jewish; slightly fewer are Belarusian. Ukraine was known as the breadbasket of the U.S.S.R., and in bumper years produced over 40 percent of the U.S.S.R.'s total agricultural output by value. It possesses almost two thirds of the former Soviet Union's coal reserves, numerous iron mines and some oil. It has produced up to 20 percent of the U.S.S.R.'s chemicals and machinery, as well as large amounts of consumer goods.

After the rise of Moscow as the political center of the Eastern Slavic world in the late Middle Ages, Ukrainian Kiev remained an important door to Europe. It provided religious leaders and artists exposed to the Western traditions that had been denied the Russians due to the self-imposed isolation of the czars. An anti-Polish revolt by the Ukrainian Cossacks in 1648 received substantial support from Moscow, and the Russian Empire thereupon absorbed Ukraine. Peter I ("the Great") repressed an anti-Russian revolt by the Ukrainian gentry in 1709; by 1783, under Catherine II (also "the Great") even Ukraine's formal autonomy within the empire

Chernobyl Makes Ukraine Want Independence

To the Editor:

Imagine having your government exhort your participation, and that of your children, in the annual parade down Main Street while, entirely unknown to you, a highly radioactive plume hung over your city, and unseen radioactive dust and ash had spread over that city's streets and sidewalks. Imagine further these same government officials, again unknown to you, having earlier evacuated columns of their own children to distant safety in secretly commandeered planes and trains.

A scene, perhaps, from a science fiction movie? To the contrary, in 1986 in my hometown, Kiev in the Ukraine, these events took place. Five days before the annual May Day parade and celebration, the Chernobyl nuclear reactor exploded some 60 miles north of Kiev. Party officials began secret evacuations of their children almost immediately, but in public statements denied that anything unusual had happened — the May Day parade had to go on as planned. And so on May 1, 1986, tens of thousands of children marched unwarned and unprotected through an environment saturated with radioactive poisons to celebrate the glories of the Communist reign.

Some of our children who marched on that fateful day or who on the days preceding it or the two weeks succeeding it played outside in our schoolyards and playgrounds are quietly dying of leukemia.

Potassium iodide prevents the absorption of radioactive iodine by the thyroid gland. It was widely available in the Soviet Union in 1986. It could have made a big difference. Protective clothing could have made a difference. Even staying inside could have made a difference. So repeatedly muses the half-mad Ukrainian mother who alternates between help less tears and frightful rage.

The democratic forces of th Ukraine ranging from Green Wor to Rukh seek independence and ful fledged democratization for the sim ple reason that neither is possibl without the other.

The Ukraine seeks democratiz tion and independence for the sam reasons Americans and countless others have sought them for centu ries: to establish a system of politic accountability, which, had it been i place in 1986, would not have allowe some children to ride trains to th Crimea while others participated in march of death down Khreshchaty the central boulevard of Kiev

Some in the United States seem think the push for sovereignty in th Soviet republics such as the Ukrain a kind of nuisance, an untimely cha lenge to a Nobel Peace Prize winne who wishes to keep the fraying em pire intact. I would invite those Amer icans to come to the Ukraine. Le them visit the mothers of the childre of Chernobyl and explain why th man who in 1986 was at the helm o the Government that played wit their children's lives with lies de serves continued support.

And let them explain to the moth ers why their children had to marcl while those of the party were evacu ated.
YURIY MISHCHENKO
ANATOLY PANOV
Kiev, U.S.S.R., April 26, 1991

The writers of the above letter to The New York Times are, respectively executive secretary and vice president o Green World (Zeleny Svit), Ukrainian Environmental Association.

was abolished. Political suppression, however, could never entirely stifle Ukrainians' consciousness of their historical and cultural distinctness from Russia.

The disastrous accident at the Chernobyl nuclear facility, located in northern Ukraine, in April 1986 triggered the contemporary movement for Ukrainian independence. An equally important factor was the historical memory of the terrible famine of the 1930s, which hit Ukraine particularly hard. The Soviet state systematically plundered the land and seized the grain for export. It "collectivized" Soviet agriculture (that is, it arbitrarily expropriated all farms). Peasants who resisted were deported or executed. Perhaps as many as 7 million Ukrainians died.

The independent Ukrainian government is headed by President Leonid M. Kravchuk, popularly elected in December 1991 and a career Communist politician prior to joining the independence movement. Kravchuk, like many of his colleagues in other republics, has embraced nationalism as the key to political survival in the post-Soviet era.

Belarus

Geography has fated Belarus (or White Russia, so-called because of its numerous white birch trees) to be the military crossroads of Eastern Europe, sandwiched historically between the Germans, Poles and Lithuanians to the west, the Swedes (a major military power in the seventeenth and early eighteenth centuries) to the north, and Russia to the east and, through control of Ukraine, to the south. Completely rebuilt after 1945, the Belarusian economy is dominated by the chemical industry. The environmental damage inflicted by chemicals was magnified by the Chernobyl disaster, which rendered 10 percent of Belarusian territory uninhabitable and up to 20 percent of its farmland unsuitable for agriculture. As with Ukraine, the accident at Chernobyl proved a catalyst in the previously dormant Belarusian nationalist movement, which had been restricted largely to literary and cultural circles. As early as July 1990, the Belarusian parliament had declared its sovereignty, stating that Belarus would be a neutral and nuclear-free state in the future.

II. The Muslims: Central Asia

Two thirds of the U.S.S.R. was located in Asia; one third of Asia was part of the U.S.S.R. An important part of that Asian patrimony is the broad swath of territory between the Chinese frontier and the Caspian Sea known as Central Asia, most of which fell within the U.S.S.R. Perceptive scholars have noted that in important respects the Middle East itself begins (or ends) in Central Asia. The nearly 50 million native peoples of the region are mainly Turkic Sunni Muslims, the prime exception being the Sunni Tajiks, bordering on China, who speak an Iranian dialect little different from Persian. Several of the Central Asian peoples, notably the Kazakhs, Kyrgyz and Tajiks, live astride the old Soviet-Chinese frontier.

Ironically, Central Asian nationalism is almost entirely the product of the Soviet period. Before 1917, tribal identification was dominant among the numerous Turkic peoples inhabiting the region. In an effort to block efforts to align the Central Asian peoples with Turkey, the Soviet authorities—once they had reconquered Central Asia as part of the greater Soviet Russian empire—instituted ethnically based administrative and political demarcations throughout the area. Thus, the Central Asian peoples were endowed with the nominal political attributes of nationhood, that is, their own states (or republics, in Soviet usage): Kazakhstan, Tajikistan, Uzbekistan, Turkmenistan, and Kyrgyzstan. Until the Russian Revolution, these peoples used the Arabic script. In a further effort to cut them off from their brethren abroad, the Soviet authorities insisted on the Latin alphabet in the 1920s. Still not satisfied, the Communists imposed the Cyrillic alphabet, unique to the Slavic world, in the 1930s.

The collapse of Soviet power has witnessed a nationalist and to a lesser degree Islamic upsurge throughout the region. At the same time, these republics' heavy economic dependence on Russia finds them paying very close attention to the course of Russian politics and economics. Governments throughout the region are dominated for the most part by ex-Communists who have embraced nationalism to survive politically. Most recently, Turkey, Iran, Pakistan and Saudi Arabia have launched direct diplomatic contacts in the region, as each seeks to promote political and religious relationships favorable to its own interests. In May 1992, several of these republics, including Kazakhstan, signed bilateral military agreements with Russia.

Kazakhstan

Kazakhstan is the second largest republic by area, about five times the size of France. Kazakhstan contains over 100 ethnic

Following the Chernobyl nuclear accident in April 1986, heliocopters measure radiation on a round-the-clock schedule.

The Bettmann Archive

groups, including 2 million Germans, who first settled along the Volga River in the time of Peter the Great (1682–1725) and were forcibly relocated to Kazakhstan by Stalin during World War II. More than 1 million of the nomadic Kazakhs, or nearly a third of the entire native population, perished in the Soviet drive to collectivize agriculture in the 1930s.

The Kazakhs themselves, racially a mixture of Turkic and Mongol peoples, are outnumbered by Russians: they constitute 36 percent of the republic's 16.5 million people, compared with the Russians' 41 percent; the Ukrainians number 6 percent. Riots in December 1986 after a Russian from outside the republic was named Communist party chief caught the Soviet and outside world by surprise, and marked the beginning of the series of nationalist challenges to Soviet rule that came to characterize the Gorbachev period.

Kazakhstan is rich in many natural resources, including coal, oil, copper, tungsten, zinc and other minerals. Nomadic pastureland in the north of the country was settled in the 1950s by Russians and Ukrainians in order to augment the U.S.S.R.'s grain production. Results have been mixed, at best. A major Soviet nuclear-test site was located in Semipalatinsk; this has since been closed at the insistence of the Kazakh parliament. A treaty to respect existing borders was signed with Russia in late August 1991.

Kazakhstan is one of four former Soviet republics in which strategic nuclear missiles are based (the others are Russia, Ukraine and Belarus): while the Kazakh government has publicly endorsed the idea of Kazakhstan as a nuclear-free zone, it has from time to time hedged on this commitment, apparently as a bargaining counter with the Russian government.

Uzbekistan

Uzbekistan, somewhat larger than California in size, is the largest Central Asian country by population, with nearly 20 million inhabitants. Of this number, about 70 percent is ethnically Uzbek and 11 percent Russian (mainly in the cities). Kazakhs, Tajiks and Tatars each represent some 4 percent. Uzbek Muslims are the third largest of the former Soviet peoples after the Russians and Ukrainians and have the strongest nationalist movement in the region. Indeed, until the advent of Russian imperial rule in the mid-nineteenth century, the Uzbeks were the ruling tribal race in Central Asia.

The Uzbek economy is dominated by cotton, which was introduced on a mass scale in the Soviet period. However, the environmental costs have been enormous: gargantuan canal projects designed to provide large-scale irrigation have drained away 40 percent of the Aral Sea, which is the water source for the entire region; indiscriminate use of pesticides is held responsible for producing an epidemic spread of throat cancer and an infant mortality rate that is among the highest in the world.

Turkmenistan

Turkmenistan, slightly larger in size than Uzbekistan, is located mainly in the Kara-Kum Desert; gas, oil and sulfur deposits have been discovered. The population of 3.5 million includes 68 percent Turkmenians, 13 percent Russians (again, mainly in the cities), 9 percent Uzbeks, and 3 percent Kazakhs. In the Murgab Valley and nearby oases, cotton, dates, olives, figs and sesame grow. Turkmenistan, which before the Russian Revolution was composed overwhelmingly of nomadic Sunni Muslim tribes, was for a long time perhaps the poorest country of the former U.S.S.R. The export of natural gas has significantly improved its prospects in recent years. Interestingly, some Western experts judge that it is precisely the lack of large-scale industry that may favor economic development in Turkmenistan. Economic policy, in this view, can concentrate on agriculture without the investment burden of many obsolete industrial plants that plagues so many other areas of the former U.S.S.R. In May 1992, Turkmenistan signed a bilateral security treaty with Russia.

Kyrgyzstan

Kyrgyzstan, the size of South Dakota and located along the Chinese border, specializes in wool and livestock production. The latter includes yaks in the Tien Shan mountains. The population of 4.3 million is divided among Kyrgyz (48 percent), Russians (26 percent), Uzbeks (12 percent), Ukrainians (2.5 percent) and Tatars (2 percent).

Tajikistan

Tajikistan, slightly smaller than Florida, is a predominantly mountainous country that borders China and has a small ethnic Tajik population. Unlike the other Central Asian peoples, the Tajiks are not Turkic but Aryan in racial origin and speak an Iranian dialect. Most of the population of 5.1 million lives in valleys of the Pamir Mountains, where cattle and sheep are raised. Various fruits are also grown, and hydroelectric power is plentiful. The population breaks down as follows: 59 percent Tajiks, 23 percent Uzbeks, 8 percent Russians and 2 percent Tatars.

III. Peoples of the Caucasus: Armenia, Azerbaijan, Georgia

The Armenians and Georgians are ancient Christian peoples, whose civilization predates that of the Russians by nearly a thousand years.

Armenia

Armenia is the smallest of the former Soviet republics, with a population of 3.3 million. Mountainous and rural, Armenia is slightly larger than Maryland. The population is 90 percent Armenian and 3 percent Azeri; Russians make up only about 2.3 percent of the total. A horrendous earthquake in December 1988, whose effects were magnified by shoddy Soviet construction standards, cost more than 25,000 lives. As a victim of the Turkish genocide of 1915–16, in which more than a million Armenians died, Armenia has looked to Soviet Russia for protection against Turkey. (Russia first conquered Armenia from Persia in 1828.) This pattern is likely to continue in the post-Soviet period, especially in light of the bloody conflict between Armenia and Turkic Muslim Azerbaijan over the Armenian enclave within Azerbaijan called Nagorno-Karabakh. Over a thousand lives have been lost and up to half a million refugees created since 1988 by fighting between Armenians and Azeris over the political fate of the Nagorno-Karabakh territory. In the spring of 1992, Armenia and Russia signed a bilateral security treaty.

Azerbaijan

Azerbaijan, the other party to the conflict, has been divided since 1907 between Russia (later the U.S.S.R.) and Iran. The larger segment remains part of Iran. Unlike the Persian Shiite Muslims, the Azeris are Turkic, although mainly (two thirds) Shiite by religious persuasion. The 1989 population of 7 million was 78 percent Azeri, 8 percent Russian, and 8 percent Armenian. The Russians live mainly in Baku, the capital, which was an oil center for the Russian Empire beginning in the late nineteenth century, while the Armenians are concentrated in Nagorno-Karabakh and Baku. Baku oil production is now only a minor fraction of the total for the former Soviet region; its refining capacity is considerably more important. The Armenian-Azeribaijani conflict over Nagorno-Karabakh has seen a significant diminution in the Armenian and Russian populations, as many have left as refugees or emigrants. Armenian armed forces had expelled Azeris from Nagorno-Karabakh by May 1992; the Azeri government has pledged to reconquer the territory, and has indicated (June 1992) that it now considers its adherence to the commonwealth null and void.

Georgia

Georgia, the third Caucasus republic, borders on the Black Sea and is in many ways a Mediterranean-like country. Georgia possesses a warm, semitropical climate, many coastal and mountain resort areas, and grew most of the U.S.S.R.'s tea, citrus fruits, grapes, silk, bamboo and tobacco. Its population of 5.5 million is composed of 69 percent Georgians, 9 percent Armenians, 7 percent Russians, 5 percent Azeris, 3 percent Ossetians, and 1.7 percent Abkhazians.

Georgia sought the protection of the Russian empress against Turkey in 1783. By 1801, Russia had annexed most of the country. Georgia experienced a brief period of independence which was proclaimed in 1918 and lasted only until 1921 when it was conquered by the Red Army and made into a Soviet republic. Since independence in 1991, Georgian leaders have resisted the efforts of the Ossetians and Abkhazians, who had their own autonomous districts under Soviet rule, to secure independence for themselves. In addition, the Georgian independence coalition led by Zviad K. Gamsakhurdia, a long-time anti-Communist dissident who had spent years in Soviet jails, split in 1991 into warring factions, as opponents charged Gamsakhurdia with adopting the stance of a dictator. Hundreds of lives have been lost in internecine Georgian conflict, with former Soviet troops standing aside ever since the massacre by Soviet troops of 20 Georgian nationalist demonstrators in the capital city of Tbilisi in April 1989. In March 1992, Eduard A. Shevardnadze, former Soviet foreign minister and before that Communist party chief in Georgia, was appointed head of state.

IV. Moldova

Moldova, which borders Romania, belonged to Romania until 1940 when Stalin's government annexed the region as a consequence of the Nazi-Soviet alliance. In order to sever connections with Romania, the Soviet Communists imposed the Cyrillic alphabet on what they called the "Moldavian" (actually Romanian) language, a Romance language closely related to French, Italian, etc. Moldova reverted to the Latin alphabet in 1989 and has been rapidly reestablishing its ties with Romania. Reunification with Romania seems inevitable, once the Romanian political situation stabilizes. Moldova contained nearly one fourth of the U.S.S.R.'s vineyards, and produces significant quantities of wine, tobacco, grain and vegetables. Its population of 4.4 million is divided among Moldovans (64 percent), Ukrainians (14 percent), Russians (13 percent), Gagauz (4 percent), Jews (2 percent) and Bulgarians (2 percent). Moldova faces secessionist movements from the Turkic-Christian Gagauzi and especially from the ethnic Russians and Ukrainians who settled along the left bank of the Dniester River, where more than half the population is Russian and Ukrainian. By the spring of 1992, siege warfare had broken out in eastern Moldova, where ethnic Russians—backed by elements of the ex-Soviet 14th Army—fought to enforce their secession from Romanian Moldova. More than 200 people had been killed and 700 wounded through the first half of 1992.

Nationalism and the Collapse of the U.S.S.R.

On December 25, 1991, the Soviet flag was lowered from atop the Kremlin, symbolizing the fact that the U.S.S.R. had now ceased to exist. Not a bang or a whimper accompanied this dramatic event, which signaled the end not just of Soviet communism but also of a nuclear superpower, one of the five permanent members of the United Nations Security Council. Any analysis of present-day U.S. foreign policy and East-West relations must begin with this astonishing fact.

The collapse of the U.S.S.R. and of its international position was a direct consequence of the internal crisis of the Soviet system, a crisis brought to its head by the efforts of President Gorbachev to save it through sweeping internal reforms. The nineteenth century French statesman Alexis de Tocqueville observed that the most dangerous moment for a bad government is when it tries to improve itself. Such was Gorbachev's experience as his reforms plunged the Soviet empire first into political and economic chaos and then into an interstate transmutation in the guise of the Commonwealth of Independent States that has put an end to the unitary Soviet party-state.

In attempting to reform what he and his closest colleagues at the time (such as Shevardnadze) recognized to be a failing economic, political and social system, Gorbachev unleashed powerful forces that were intended to support his reform efforts. Instead, in the absence of sufficient consensus on basic political values, they rapidly moved far beyond the point where Gorbachev or anyone else could easily control or influence them. Gorbachev repeatedly had to accommodate forces that he originally did not intend to countenance, at first in order to keep the momentum of reform moving, and later in order to preserve a union whose existence the reform process itself had come to threaten. He thus came by 1990–91 to find himself on the horns of a most painful dilemma: he could attempt to preserve the traditional, centralized union by coercion, in which case he would lose all chance of reform (to which he nevertheless remained committed), or he could compromise with the forces of republican sovereignty, as personified by Yeltsin. But since these forces were pursuing genuine independence from the union, such a compromise would really be a capitulation and lead to the end of the U.S.S.R. as history had known it. The dramatic failed coup of August 19–21, 1991, resolved Gorbachev's dilemma in favor of the latter choice, i.e., the end of the Soviet state and with it the president's own political career.

How did this situation come about? So much has happened so quickly since the outset of the Gorbachev era in 1985 that there is a tendency to forget the reasons for the bold reforms pushed by Gorbachev and the plausibility, to both Soviet and Western observers at that time, of structural reform of the Soviet system. (As Seweryn Bialer and Joan Afferica wrote in *Foreign Affairs,* "The Soviet Union…boasts enormous unused reserves of political and social stability that suffice to endure the deepest difficulties.")

Briefly stated, the system that Gorbachev inherited in March 1985 faced what he euphemistically continued to call for several years a precrisis situation. Growth rates in the economy had been declining steadily and dramatically since the early 1960s. In the early 1980s the U.S.S.R. had, by Gorbachev's admission, experienced an economic depression. The result, while not yet a challenge to the survival of the Soviet system, imposed fundamental limitations upon the ability of the government to attain its declared domestic and foreign policy objectives. The trade-offs between military spending, foreign policy commitments, investment in heavy civilian industry, in light civilian industry, in agriculture and in civilian consumption were becoming increasingly painful, affecting the performance of the Soviet system and even the sources of stability of the system at home and abroad. Western economists estimate that the portion of the Soviet economy devoted to consumption was actually smaller than that allocated by Nazi Germany during World War II, at less than 50 percent of the total. Even the long-term ability of the Soviet military to maintain forces competitive with those of the United States in a high-technology environment was called into question, transforming many in the Soviet armed forces into advocates of economic reform.

The social consequences of this economic bind were dramatic. No growth in the economy meant little improvement in social services and a standard of living that had long been starved by the Soviet preoccupation with the military and heavy-industry sectors. Male life expectancy had declined from a high of 68 years in the mid-1960s to 62 years by the early 1980s, an unprecedented development in peacetime for an industrially developed country. Up to 40 percent of male deaths in recent years have been of working-age men (i.e., age 60 or under), primarily due to environmental contamination, unsafe workplaces and alcoholism. The U.S.S.R. by the early 1980s was experiencing infant mortality rates which put it at No. 50 in the world, behind Barbados and Kuwait.

Yet, this was not all. International developments were causing comparable concern. The eruption of the Polish crisis in 1980–81 sent shudders throughout the Soviet leadership as it witnessed the disintegration of the authority of the Polish Communist party in the face of the workers' movement represented by Solidarity. The message was clear even to the most diehard reactionaries: as Soviet President Konstantin U. Chernenko (1984–85) himself observed, the Polish crisis presented a negative object lesson of what happens when a Communist party loses contact with the masses. If the Soviet system were to avoid a similar fate, long festering social, economic and even political problems could no longer be ignored.

In its relationships with key countries outside the bloc, the U.S.S.R. was increasingly isolated. Having failed to prevent deployment of Pershing II nuclear missiles in Western Europe, the

U.S.S.R. at the end of 1983 suspended arms-control negotiations with the United States on both intermediate- and intercontinental-range nuclear forces. This step did no harm to the American position or to the political viability of key American allies in Western Europe. The "bleeding wound" (Gorbachev's term) of Afghanistan was demoralizing Soviet society further and complicating Moscow's relations with a number of Third World countries, especially in the Islamic world. Relations with China remained essentially frozen. In the Middle East, continued Soviet refusal to deal with Israel ensured the U.S. position as the privileged interlocutor for Arabs and Israelis alike, thus shutting the U.S.S.R. out of the "peace process" in the region. At the same time the Soviet leadership found itself supporting poor and increasingly threatened regimes in Angola, Ethiopia, Mozambique and Nicaragua (not to mention Afghanistan and Cuba, the latter alone costing the U.S.S.R. several million dollars per day). These foreign and domestic challenges came together with magnified force as a result of the computer/information revolution, led by the world's two largest, dynamic (and capitalist) economies, the United States and Japan. They came at a time when the Soviet economy that had never mastered even its first industrial revolution was in full crisis and facing an American defense buildup—especially the Strategic Defense Initiative—which promised to produce an unbearable strain upon Soviet resources and a possible revolution in the strategic-nuclear balance.

Gorbachev's Reforms Justified

Such was the situation facing Gorbachev in 1985 and the justification for glasnost and *perestroika* (restructuring the economy by decentralizing decisionmaking) that became his hallmark. The decision to embark on such far-reaching reforms was hardly a unique one in the sweep of Russian history. Imperial reformers throughout Russian history tried, with varying degrees of success, to modernize and rationalize Russian society through ambitious economic, administrative and cultural campaigns. Their aim was to mobilize society to the purposes of the state and in the process to imbue a rigid autocratic system of rule with dynamism and creativity. In the end, none of the czars was prepared to renounce the autocratic principle and accept the elite classes as independent forces in society. Czar Alexander III (1881–94) believed that the advent of constitutional government would mean the end of the multinational empire. Outside of the autocratic principle, there was no evident way of binding together the diverse nations that made up the Russian (and later Soviet) Empire.

Amazingly, Gorbachev seems not to have judged the multinational composition of the Soviet state to have been an important consideration in his decisions to make reforms in 1985. Time and again, from 1985 through late 1987, Gorbachev approved of Communist party declarations to the effect that the historical problem of relations between the nations of the U.S.S.R. had been "resolved" once and for all. In Kiev, capital of Ukraine, the largest and most important of the non-Russian republics of the Soviet Union, Gorbachev twice in the same 1985 speech identified "Russians" with Soviets, indicating a phenomenal blindness to the multinational aspect of the Soviet system. In this sense, Gorbachev overlooked a consideration that had repeatedly stayed the hand of past reformers. He therefore proceeded along a path of progressively more-radical reform, which he thought could revive a failing system. Reconstructing the record of the period 1985–88, it appears that Gorbachev never considered that the discrediting and dismantling of the old, neo-Stalinist structures of power and values would encourage the emergence of nationalist claims whose logical consequence would be to threaten the very union that the policies of perestroika and glasnost were designed to strengthen. For the Gorbachev of 1985, the chief threat to the U.S.S.R. was the long-term prospect of its decline to the status of a second-rank power because of its inability to assimilate the global revolution in computers, information and communications.

In this light, the "early" Gorbachev did understand, as did the imperial reformers in their time, that the system itself had reached an impasse in its development. Only a basic change in the workings of the system—akin to Peter the Great's opening to the West, Alexander II's abolition of serfdom (1861), or Piotr Stolypin's (Nicholas II's prime minister) 1910 gamble on making landowners out of peasants—could rejuvenate it and maintain the Soviet Union's international position and prestige. For Gorbachev, this meant at first reducing the administrative apparatus for running the economy and giving far greater latitude to material incentive and individual initiative in the economy and the affairs of society. In order to promote this program, Gorbachev began by reaching out to society, in the first instance the technical and creative intelli-

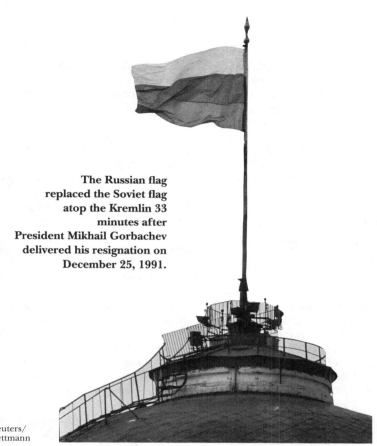

The Russian flag replaced the Soviet flag atop the Kremlin 33 minutes after President Mikhail Gorbachev delivered his resignation on December 25, 1991.

Reuters/
Bettmann

gentsia, in an attempt to recruit the voluntary allegiance of "the best and the brightest" the U.S.S.R. had to offer. If he was to break the comfortable inertia that many in the country had come to value after the upheavals of the early Soviet period, Gorbachev had to offer those best qualified to modernize the system good reason to collaborate with him. This implied higher salaries for the able, greater professional latitude for the Soviet "white-collar class," and more freedom of expression for the creative intelligentsia. In effect, Gorbachev was trying to create the kind of dynamic civil society that all reformers since Peter the Great had tried to encourage but ultimately proved unwilling to accept.

It is now clear, and Gorbachev has admitted as much, that the

110118

Soviet reform leadership did not take the full measure of the economic crisis afflicting the country or the depth of popular apathy. In part, this was due to inadequate information, especially on the state of the economy. Decades of willful deception in reporting on mandatory plan fulfillments had led to the point where no one in the system, including perhaps most of the top leadership, had an accurate picture of the state and direction of the Soviet economy. More important still, the Soviet leadership, and in the first instance Gorbachev himself, was neither able nor willing to come to terms with the profound disaffection from the Soviet system that had set in among the population in general and had long been present among some of the non-Russian nations of the Soviet Union.

The consequence of this curious appraisal of the state of the union, one that was both candid and naive, was a concerted effort by Gorbachev and his allies to make a rapid transition from a neo-Stalinist political and economic system to a more traditional but still authoritarian system. They appeared confident that there were enough unused reserves and at least passive consensus in the system to tide them over the dangerous initial stage of reform. The first years of the Gorbachev period were thus characterized by the pell-mell dismantling of the Leninist-Stalinist institutions of state and party power, and, as important, of the Leninist-Stalinist version of Russian and Soviet history, before either could be replaced. As a result, the Gorbachev leadership soon found itself in a quandary: where it did not encounter apathy due to the success of the Soviet system in destroying personal initiative, public spirit and trust in government, it confronted nationalists who may have approved of his overall concept of reform but who were determined to expropriate it for their own ends. The central tenets of Leninism—the ideology of the single truth and political institutions based on a monopoly of power—had been destroyed. Except for nationalism, no political force has yet emerged to replace them.

Gorbachev did prove himself capable of destroying the old Stalinist institutional and psychological order founded on repression and fear. For that alone, he will go down in history. Yet by late 1990 it became evident that Gorbachev was not the man to replace the old system with a viable alternative. The amazing political comeback of Yeltsin, expelled from the Soviet Politburo with

Gorbachev's approval in February 1988, and the appearance of other nationalist leaders throughout the non-Russian republics of the U.S.S.R.—each insisting on sovereign independence from the Soviet state—represented a dramatic defeat for Gorbachev's reformist concept, which was designed to preserve a strong, centralized U.S.S.R., not bury it. Yet the emergence of these new forces was a natural reaction to the inability of the existing power structure, Gorbachev included, to elicit broad support for saving the Soviet system.

Civil War?

This collapse of authority within the U.S.S.R., as evidenced by the breakdown of the Soviet economic and political systems and the general rejection of Gorbachev's rule, has led many observers within and outside the Soviet Union to predict the onset of civil war throughout the land, with corresponding international consequences. What is the probability of such a denouement?

One element usually associated with revolutionary and/or civil explosions, which historically has proved a necessary and even sufficient condition for the outbreak of sustained mass civil violence, has not been present in the current Soviet political equation, namely, an open schism within the military and the paramilitary. Such a schism would lead the various factions to take up opposing sides, appeal to powerful, sympathetic forces in society, and use force, with the likely death of thousands. The curious and abortive coup against the Baltic states in January 1991 had already suggested considerable hesitancy about the massive use of force. In retrospect, it seems clear that the failure of repressive measures in the Baltic lands emboldened the general Soviet population. The consequent ability of the Moscow population to confront the August 1991 coup in the streets, in the manner of the East European revolutions of 1989, posed an awful dilemma for the Soviet Army: on the one hand, a massive use of force would be required in order to dissuade the population from further challenges to its authority; on the other hand, the military leadership could not be certain that orders to conscripted soldiers to use force against civilian populations would be obeyed. There was the possibility that a break in the military's ranks—as happened in Yugoslavia in June and July 1991—might actually precipitate its disintegration. This is an outcome which neither soldiers nor politicians nor political scientists can predict. It was a test that those plotting the Soviet coup preferred, happily, to avoid.

Perhaps the most powerful moderating factor today is the Soviet peoples' pervasive sense that civil war *is* a real possibility. Having experienced unparalleled collective tragedy in this century, from wars and occupations to revolution, famines, purges, deportations and mass imprisonment, not to mention three years of civil war just after the 1917 revolution, the peoples of the former Soviet Union, most of all the Slavic peoples, simply have no tolerance for the misery and suffering that revolutionary and civil violence entail. They are afraid and exhausted. In this respect, the very threat of civil war acts as a deterrent. Furthermore, the various Soviet peoples share, as a matter of collective consciousness, the common experience and memory of oppression by Stalinism and its political legacy. That is, the Russians, Ukrainians, Belarusians (and even the Baltic peoples) share a community of fate (absent in the case of the Yugoslav peoples) that works against the generalized expression of political-ethnic violence. To the extent that Yeltsin is able to continue to recast the political vocation of the Russian nation in a nonimperial direction, the prospects for civil peace throughout the former U.S.S.R. can only increase.

By all accounts, the military, especially after the chastening experience of the August 1991 coup, has little inclination as a corporate body to shoulder the unhappy responsibilities that political intervention and governance today would bring. Furthermore, as the August 1991 events have shown, few citizens would support a junta, regardless of its political orientation, that seized power. There is, in addition, no identifiable civilian agency or personality outside of the nationalist reform movements that seems ready, willing and able to address the crisis besetting the post-Soviet region as a whole and around whom elements of the military might rally. The military will now have to accommodate themselves to those forces, led by Yeltsin, that can credibly promise a strong Russia. This would follow the precedent of the early 1920s, which found many former czarist officers rallying to the Bolsheviks (ideological antipathies aside) as the last hope for a strong Russian state. This assessment appears to have been confirmed by the unprecedented convocation of some 5,000 military officers in Moscow in mid-January 1992. While giving vent to their frustration at the disintegration of the Soviet Union and thus the obsolescence of all Soviet institutions, including the military, the officers rejected the few open threats that were made, as well as any hint of nostalgia for Communist power. Officers repeatedly insisted that they would never take arms "against the people" and, most importantly, Commonwealth Defense Minister Marshal I. Yevgeny Shaposhnikov acknowledged that the post-Soviet states have the right to form their own national armies. The officers' final resolution asked only for a limited transitional period that would preserve common security institutions and provide for a stable redistribution of former Soviet military resources. The establishment of a Russian Ministry of Defense in March 1992, with Yeltsin as acting defense minister, seemed to cast the die in the direction of national military establishments. In May 1992, Yeltsin appointed General Pavel Grachev, whose support was crucial in defeating the August 1991 coup, as the Russian Minister of Defense.

The Russian Federation:
Nation-State or Empire?

President Yeltsin is the first leader in Russian history to break with the imperial pattern of politics. For most of its history, the rulers of Russia have ruled over large numbers of non-Russians, whether in the Russian Empire or in the U.S.S.R. Indeed, while Russians made up a slight majority in the latter-day U.S.S.R., ethnic Russians were just 44 percent of the population of imperial Russia, according to the census of 1897. The task of managing a multinational empire has always framed the political choices before the Russian and Soviet Russian leadership. In some respects, the appeal of such transnational ideologies as pan-Slavism and communism itself reflected the need of Russian leaders to develop a political rationale that did not rest on an exclusively nationalist identification with Russians, thereby excluding the non-Russian half of the population.

As has been noted, another political consequence of the multinational character of the historical Russian state has been to limit the scope of reforms designed to modernize the country. Yeltsin has based his rise to power in Russia in part on the argument that Russian imperialism actually acts to the detriment of the interests of the Russian people. First, the need to control large non-Russian populations requires a dictatorship that is as oppressive to the Russians as it is to the non-Russians. Second, the equally compelling need to offer inducements to disloyal non-Russian subjects to collaborate in imperial rule requires a degree of economic subsidy from Russia that the already impoverished Russian people can ill afford.

Emergence of Russian National Consciousness

Yeltsin drew on a ground swell of popular and elite dissatisfaction with Soviet treatment of Russian interests. In the late 1980s, there had grown in Russia a movement to establish specifically Russian institutions in the political and educational areas, on the argument that existing Soviet institutions subordinated Russian interests to those of the union as a whole. Paradoxically, while many abroad held that the absence of a specifically Russian Communist party or a Russian Academy of Sciences only proved that the counterpart Soviet institutions were really Russian at heart, increasing numbers of Russians began to perceive that the Soviet state had systematically hindered the development of powerful Russian political institutions out of fear that they would attract Russians away from the Soviet system.

It was the writer Alexander I. Solzhenitsyn who first elaborated the contemporary Russian nationalist critique of the Soviet system in his 1973 book, *Letter to the Soviet Leaders*. Solzhenitsyn argued that the Soviet system had led Russia to a fateful decline due to the political, economic, cultural, moral, demographic and environmental trauma that communism had inflicted on the country. In brief, Solzhenitsyn contended that the Soviet leaders had used the Russian people as guinea pigs for a grotesque political experiment and that the consequences—tens of millions killed in and out of the gulags, or labor camps, the destruction of the countryside due to the violent collectivization of agriculture, the impoverishment of the population, the destruction of the Russian church and with it the collapse of Russian culture and morals, the reckless exploitation of Russia's natural resources and ensuing environmental contamination, and the long-term decline of the Russian population in terms of numbers and health—all heralded a catastrophe for the Russian people. Some way had to be found to represent Russian interests at the level of national politics. For Solzhenitsyn and others after him this meant, first, relinquishing those parts of the Soviet Empire—especially in underdeveloped Muslim Central Asia—that represented a drain on Russian economic and political development, and second, asserting Russian national control over the country's destiny.

A remarkable group of Russian writers who emerged in the mid-1960s focused in particular on the destruction of the Russian countryside as a symbol of the fate of Russia under Soviet rule. Only with the advent of greater political openness under Gorbachev did the viewpoint of these writers, known as the *derevenshchiki* ("village prose" writers), assume specific political significance. After 1985 they and their political allies concentrated on three fronts: first, on saving vast Russian territories from inundation by opposing the planned redirection of Siberian rivers to Central Asia (the project was rapidly cancelled after the intervention of the distinguished historian Dmitrii Likhachev); second, on resurrecting the truth about the genocide of the Russian and Ukrainian peasantry during the 1930s (previously classified census materials from the 1930s bore out the most pessimistic estimates of more than 10 million killed during collectivization); and, finally, on raising the question of how and why this could have happened to Russia.

The resulting nationalist discussion, curiously, did not assume a superior or exclusionary tone directed against other peoples, but rather became infused with the sentiments of pain and humiliation—a searching within the Russian nation for the sources of its rebirth. The more systematic and public analysis of Russia's plight afforded by glasnost yielded some dramatic findings. Together with the three Baltic states, Russia had suffered the highest mortality rate of the U.S.S.R. In the educational field, Russians appeared to have been discriminated against in favor of other, non-Russian nations of the U.S.S.R. By the 1970s Russia had on average less than half as many institutions of higher learning in proportion to population as the rest of the Soviet republics, and only a fifth as many members of the Academy of Sciences in relation to population.The Russian people did not exist as such in Soviet history. Nor, consequently, was there an institution for the defense of the Russian language, which in many respects had been reduced to its lowest common denominator through its transformation into the lingua franca of the multinational former Soviet Union.

The national discussion about Russia's fate in the Soviet period led by 1990 to the establishment of specifically Russian or Russian-oriented cultural institutions. The new Patriarch of the Russian Orthodox Church, Alexis II, gave the church's benediction to these efforts, in addition to reviving the church's own role in Russian education, culture and society. A Russian Academy of Sciences and an independent Russian Communist party—composed largely of reactionary opponents of the reforms that Gorbachev had been implementing through the Soviet Communist party—had been founded by 1990. The widespread conclusion that the Soviet system had systematically suppressed the national interests of the Russian people provided fertile cultural ground for the political exploitation of Russian nationalism. This nationalism was to propel Yeltsin to the Russian presidency by free and direct election and eventually to force Gorbachev's resignation.

Yeltsin and Russian Political Nationalism

Much of the international discussion of Russian nationalism has viewed it in alarmist terms, likening it to chauvinism or xenophobia. It is therefore important to make clear what is meant by the term. Nationalism in its political expression has historically meant the claim by a particular nation to construct its own state, i.e., a nation-state. By this standard, there has never been an effective political expression of Russian nationalism: the Russian state, in czarist and Soviet times, assumed an imperial aspect by virtue of its rule over a multinational empire. Russia's historical vocation has always been defined in transnational, rather than strictly nationalist, terms. A purely nationalist definition of the Russian interest would have constrained the development of the Russian state to those regions where ethnic Russians constituted a large majority. Russian expansionism thereby implies an imperial rather than nationalist political program for the Russian nation.

What is striking about recent Russian political development is the extent to which Russian nationalism has been advanced at the expense of Russia's historically imperial vocation. Russian President Yeltsin consented to Baltic independence in January 1991, ratifying Lithuanian independence by treaty as early as July 1991. Similarly, the newly independent Russian Federation has gladly consented to independence for the more than 50 million Turkic

Muslims of former Soviet Central Asia and has agreed to live with an independent Ukraine, considered even by many Russian liberals to be part and parcel of the Russian patrimony.

While contemporary Russian nationalism contains several diverse strands of opinion, they all had in common, from 1986 to 1990, four demands which together constituted the core of the Russian nationalist political agenda: (1) an independent Russian government; (2) the reestablishment of an independent, landed peasantry; (3) genuine separation of church and state; and (4) the restitution of traditional Russian names to cities and streets. Apart from these, the several tendencies of Russian nationalism have diverged on such important issues as the model for social-economic development (Western or some more traditional Russian model) and relations with other nations neighboring Russia and within Russia itself.

The critical first test of the political orientation of Russian nationalism came during the first round of voting for the Russian Congress of People's Deputies in March 1990. The liberals emerged surprisingly strong. At the first session of the congress on May 16, 1990, Yeltsin contested outgoing Russian Premier Aleksandr V. Vlasov for the presidency, a position which at that time had very limited powers, arguing for total Russian sovereignty versus Vlasov's "economic sovereignty in the context of the Soviet political system." Yeltsin prevailed on the third ballot by a vote of 535 to 467.

Yeltsin's first pronouncements as Russian president reflected the influence of the Russian nationalist agenda, both in promoting his astounding political comeback after being dismissed from the Soviet Politburo in early 1988 and in establishing Russia as a counterweight to Gorbachev's Soviet state. They included: (1) 100 days to establish full Russian sovereignty; (2) introduction of a presidential system of government in Russia, so that the Russian leader could deal with the Soviet leader from a position of strength; (3) rapid economic reforms, so as to move Russia ahead of the U.S.S.R. in this respect; and (4) the restitution to the Russian Orthodox Church of its full moral authority, especially in the educational system.

Having in effect proclaimed the existence of the Russian nation-state, Yeltsin and his supporters still left many important questions unanswered. Britain and France could lose their colonial empires and still remain cohesive nation-states. Could the same be said of Russia? Defining the character of the Russian future is immensely difficult. Can it secede from empire while remaining multiethnic and open to other cultures? The problem contains a monumental historical irony for Russia, for having seceded from the U.S.S.R., it now faces within its own borders the problem of ethnic and regional disintegration that—with decisive assistance from Russia itself—brought the Soviet system down.

The Structure of the Russian Federation

Several parallels may be drawn between the nominally federal structure of the U.S.S.R. and the ethnic-administrative structure of the Russian Federation. The U.S.S.R. was composed of 15 ethnically defined union republics, of which the Russian Republic was the largest; the Russian Federation, apart from its 55 geographically defined regions, contains 20 ethnically based autonomous republics.

During the winter of 1991–92, the Russian authorities presented a Federal Treaty to these autonomous republics in order to define the scope of their powers under the proposed new Russian constitution. Their hope was to avoid the ethnically based centrifugal pressures that had undermined the federal Soviet government. By March 31, 1992, 18 of the 20 autonomous republics had signed the federal treaty, which was supposed to be considered an integral part of the new Russian constitution. The treaty's main provisions include:

(1) The federal government is responsible for foreign policy, defense, defending civil rights and protecting ethnic minorities; defining federal policy for the social, political and economic development of the Russian Federation; establishing the foundations for a common market, financial and monetary policy, customs regulations, a federal budget and taxation policy; running federal energy, transport and communications systems.

(2) Shared responsibilities between the federal government, the republics and the regions include: ensuring that legislation is in accordance with the constitution; law enforcement; management, use and ownership of land, minerals and other natural resources; common matters of health, education, and culture.

(3) Republics are responsible for every other area except those they have delegated to the Russian Federation.

(4) Disputes are to be resolved through specified conciliation procedures.

(5) Russian is the official language of the federation, although republics may have their own official language.

The formal jurisdiction of the Russian Federation ends at Russia's frontiers with its commonwealth neighbors and the broader international community. The politics of Russian nationalism dictate, however, that any Russian leader take into account the fate of the more than 25 million Russians who live outside the borders of Russia proper in the republics of the former U.S.S.R.

The complications that this widespread intermingling of populations could entail are virtually endless. How Russia and its neighbors handle the potentially explosive issue of the treatment of national minorities and borders will largely determine the prospects for a peaceful transition to new political and economic principles in the successor-states to the U.S.S.R. The Russian-Lithuanian treaty of July 1991, wherein Russia recognized Lithuanian statehood and boundaries in exchange for Lithuanian guarantees of the civil rights of Russians living in the country, resolved a critical bilateral problem for Russia and could serve as a model for other troubled relationships. The Yugoslav civil war of 1991–92, triggered by Serbian and Croatian disagreement over the status of Serbians living in Croatia, stands as an object lesson and underscores the stakes which Russia and all of its neighbors have in the peaceful development of post-Soviet politics.

By late 1991, the government of the Russian Federation had embarked upon a series of unique experiments in Russian political history: the establishment of a Russian nation-state, the codification of nonimperial principles for governing relations with its immediate Slavic and Central Asian neighbors, in the form of the Commonwealth of Independent States; and the development of a constitutional political order at home, replete with multiple political parties and a proposed new constitution establishing and governing relations among new executive, legislative, judicial and federal institutions. Among the most important problems which the young government faced in early 1992 was to establish its ability to govern in the face of an ongoing economic depression and a remarkable political vacuum. Until the unexpectedly quick disintegration of the Soviet government, Russian political energies had been consumed almost entirely in opposing the policies and direction of the Soviet government, as distinct from charting those of its own. The collapse of the Soviet system thus also shortened the time that Russian politicians thought they had to arrange for a relatively stable transfer of authority from the U.S.S.R. to the Russian Federation.

Russia and the Commonwealth: Political Developments

The preamble to the pact establishing the Commonwealth of Independent States declares "that the U.S.S.R. as a subject of international law and a geopolitical reality is ceasing to exist." After affirming their general intent to preserve mutually beneficial relations on the basis of international law, the 11 former republics committed themselves, inter alia, to equal treatment of all citizens, regardless of nationality, in accordance with recognized international norms of human rights (Article 1); to protect the rights of national minorities (Article 2); maintain comprehensive cooperation among themselves (Article 4); to "recognize and respect each other's territorial integrity and the inviolability of existing frontiers" (Article 5); to "preserve and maintain under joint command a common military-strategic space, including unified control over nuclear weapons"(Article 6); to pursue joint action through "common coordinating institutions" in the spheres of foreign policy, economic policy, transport and communications, the environment, migration, and the fight against organized crime (Article 7); and to guarantee "the fulfillment of the international obligations ensuing for them from the treaties and agreements of the former U.S.S.R." (Article 12).

In fact, by May 1992 there had been little coordination among the commonwealth partners outside the sphere of strategic nuclear weapons, which it was recognized would be a Russian monopoly. This is hardly surprising, since the commonwealth possesses none of the attributes of a state, or even of normal intergovernmental agencies. The commonwealth has no capital—Minsk has simply been agreed upon as a convenient meeting place for certain purposes. Its only two coordinating bodies, the councils of heads of state and heads of government, meet only during summit meetings and, in the absence of a formal decisionmaking procedure, rely upon the unanimity principle. Perhaps most importantly, there is no permanent secretariat for the commonwealth to establish agendas or implement decisions. Almost immediately upon signing the agreement, Ukrainian President Kravchuk made clear his interpretation that the commonwealth was at most a transitional arrangement for liquidating the assets of the former U.S.S.R. so as to permit Ukraine to achieve full political and economic independence as rapidly as possible.

Russia for its part appeared determined to proceed on its own path of economic reform regardless of the hesitations of its partners. Indeed, given their extremely high degree of economic dependence on Russia, its commonwealth partners were obliged to follow suit by way of protecting their economies from dislocations in the Russian behemoth. As with the question of borders, the key to a harmonious set of commonwealth relationships will be the extent to which Russia can exercise restraint and discretion in dealing with its neighbors and, conversely, whether its neighbors—above all Ukraine—can accept a powerful Russia as long as it refrains from imperial tendencies.

Proposed Russian Constitution

The Russian Federation faces the identical problem that in the end defeated Gorbachev in his effort to reform and save the Soviet system: how to maintain the integrity of a federal state by reorganizing the division of power within it. Since the existing constitution was recognized to be inadequate for the task of constructing a new democratic Russian nation-state, Yeltsin proposed adoption of a new, Western-style constitution. In the fall of 1991 Yeltsin secured from parliament the right to rule by decree. Yeltsin furthermore added the responsibility of premier to his presidential duties in order to impart a decisive impulse to his radical economic reform, announced in late October 1991 and begun on January 2, 1992. He also postponed the election of regional governors scheduled for the end of 1991 and secured the approval of parliament to appoint these officials personally.

The proposed new constitution—which has yet to be formally considered by the Russian parliament—would eliminate the existing parliamentary framework, in which a relatively small legislature, the Supreme Soviet (152 members), conducts day-to-day business while a much larger group, the Congress of People's Deputies (1,068 members), meets occasionally as the supreme arbiter of legislation. The proposed new system is modeled on the American example and provides for a lower house, the State Duma, with 300 members directly elected on the basis of population, and an upper house, the Federal Assembly, with three delegates from each republic or province. As in the American Congress, each chamber would pass laws separately.

As for the executive branch, the Russian presidency would lose its largely ceremonial character (Yeltsin has governed largely by decree and through his personal cabinet under emergency powers) and receive clear powers comparable to the French or the American presidency. The proposed constitution preserves the nominally federal character of the Russian state while at the same time laying the institutional and political foundation to preserve what its preamble calls "the historically evolved state unity" of the "multinational people of the Russian Federation."

Russian Economic Policy

On January 2, 1992, the Russian government, under the economic guidance of now Acting Prime Minister Yegor T. Gaidar, instituted a dramatic and comprehensive set of measures aimed at stabilizing the overall economy and laying the groundwork for an effectively functioning market economy. The state of the Russian economy following the collapse of the U.S.S.R. was deplorable by any measure. The Soviet gross national product (GNP) had declined by about 17 percent in 1991, the worst economic performance recorded in Soviet history and significantly lower than the worst year of the American depression of the 1930s. Energy production and oil exports, a key earner of foreign currency, had declined even faster, and there were no appreciable increases in energy efficiency or reductions in domestic consumption to offset the decline. Food production, while not approaching famine levels, was nevertheless in serious decline, with a 1991 harvest about 25 percent lower than in 1990. By late 1991, before most price controls were lifted, the Russian economy was suffering an inflation rate of 650 to 700 percent. As a consequence, Russian living standards, never high when compared to those of Europe, declined dramatically, with more than 60 percent of Moscovites being pushed below the official poverty line. (About 90 percent would be pushed below the statistical poverty line in the first months of the Yeltsin reforms.)

On the international front, the U.S.S.R. had accumulated a hard-currency debt of nearly $90 billion by 1991, with no evident means of early repayment. (By 1992 Russia had assumed prime responsibility for paying off this debt.) The ruble, which throughout the Gorbachev period had been fixed at near parity with the dollar, collapsed to more than 100 rubles per dollar by late 1991. The fiscal system had also been seriously weakened, as the Soviet government resorted to printing money to finance expenditures not covered by taxes, which themselves had dried up in the wake of the rise of the republics to sovereign power. The amount of money in circulation increased by 63 percent in the first 11 months of 1991 (compared to 21 percent in all of 1990), and may well have doubled for the entire year.

Gaidar Reform

Faced with this legacy, which showed no signs of abating in 1992, the Russian government decided to give the economy "shock therapy" comparable to that implemented in Poland following the collapse of the Communist system there in 1989. The so-called Gaidar reform is based on three economic policies: (1) the creation of market institutions and conditions through privatization and liberalization of the price system and foreign trade; (2) the establishment of a social "safety net" for those groups most likely to suffer as a result of the rapid reforms; and (3) the imposition of licensing requirements on the export of energy and raw materials. Whereas traditional economic theory implied that price liberalization should follow macroeconomic stabilization and the privatization of the economy, so as to avoid pressures for hyperinflation in an economy still dominated by monopolies, Gaidar argued forcefully that prices should be freed first, so as to impose budgetary constraints on firms and reduce state subsidies. Without price liberalization, it was difficult to see how goods could return to the store shelves. At the same time, Russian economists anticipated a further inflation of 300 to 500 percent following the freeing of prices.

By mid-June 1992, certain signs of improvement were detectable: the nation had survived the winter without the feared starvation, the supply of goods was slowly beginning to improve, and the Russian government seemed finally to have constrained the previously chaotic printing of rubles. Deficit spending appeared to have been brought under greater control. On the other hand, less than 3 percent of agricultural land had been privatized by March 1992: in the long term, greater agricultural productivity is a precondition for successful economic reform. In early March 1992, Gaidar presented the rest of his economic reform package to parliament. It envisages the virtual elimination of the budget deficit by the end of 1992, the reduction of inflation to Western standards by the same date, and a single rate of exchange for the ruble within months. Pensions and insurance benefits are to be maintained at existing levels, but not indexed to inflation. On June 15, 1992, immediately before departing for his Washington summit meeting with President Bush, Yeltsin underlined his commitment to economic reform by promoting Gaidar to Acting Prime Minister (from First Deputy Prime Minister) and passing two decrees, over the head of a reluctant parliament, establishing bankruptcy laws and permitting the private purchase of land for industrial development.

Foreign and Defense Policy

The disintegration of the U.S.S.R. has had profound consequences for the international position of Russia. Deprived of its empire in Eastern Europe as well as at home, the rulers of Russia can no longer lay plausible claim to global political equality with the United States. For the first time in centuries, the Russian state has no common border with the heart of Europe. For the foreseeable future, its political energies will be almost entirely absorbed with preserving its political and territorial integrity, with little inclination for ambitious international enterprises. Indeed, the general assumption underlying current Russian foreign policy is the abandonment of past ideological competition with the West and instead the active cultivation of the West as a political, economic and even military ally. Specifically, the Russian leadership seeks to exploit its foreign relations to maximize international support for Russian domestic reform, even if this requires important adaptations in the reform program itself.

The foreign policy of Russia now extends to relations with its partners, who participate in the commonwealth as equals under international law. All of the former Soviet republics have been admitted to the United Nations. Russia itself has succeeded to the seat on the United Nations Security Council occupied by the U.S.S.R. Russian Foreign Minister Andrei V. Kozyrev has defined Russia's international interests in relation to its commonwealth neighbors as follows: unified commonwealth control over strategic nuclear weapons; general observance of internationally recognized

49

human rights throughout the commonwealth; the protection of Russians and the Russian-speaking population living outside of Russia throughout the commonwealth; and mutually beneficial economic cooperation. Faced with ultranationalist pressure in the Russian parliament, Kozyrev has conceded that Russia's borders might be changed, but only according to CSCE principles that this be done through negotiation and with the consent of all parties involved. Upon his return from North America on June 21, 1992, Yeltsin declared that Russia reserved the right to intervene in other former Soviet republics where negotiations had broken down and Russian "lives, property, or rights" were threatened. He made specific reference to Moldova and Ossetia, a territory split between Russia and Georgia.

Russia and Ukraine

The most important achievement to date in Russian foreign policy has been the willingness of the Russian government to live with an independent Ukraine and to deal with Ukraine as a sovereign state under international law. This has not prevented numerous difficulties from arising in Russian-Ukrainian relations, but it has prevented those differences from spilling over into open conflict between the two. Since 1990, Russia and Ukraine have three times officially affirmed their respect for the inviolability of existing frontiers. Ukraine's determined drive for independence includes the establishment of an independent Ukrainian army. This would appear to condemn the prospects for a powerful commonwealth military establishment, as each of the former Soviet republics, including Russia, seem destined to establish national armed forces. Ukraine cooperated in the transfer of tactical and strategic nuclear weapons to Russia. Ukrainian presidential adviser Volodymr Vasilenko has even put forward a nationalist rationale for the denuclearization of Ukraine: since it is technically impossible for Ukraine to operate strategic nuclear forces without Russian cooperation, Ukraine can only secure its strategic independence by relinquishing all control over such weapons. In mid-March 1992, Ukraine halted the transfer of short-range tactical nuclear weapons to Russia on the argument that there were not sufficient guarantees for the security of these weapons, either in transit or in Russia itself. It has not, however, repudiated its formal commitment to become a nuclear-free state. (The same holds for

Kazakhstan and Belarus, the other republics outside of Russia where strategic nuclear forces remain based.) By May 1992, after expressions of concern by the United States, Ukraine had apparently completed the shipment of tactical nuclear weapons to Russia and reaffirmed its commitment to nonnuclear status and—together with Belarus and Kazakhstan—agreed to sign the 1968 Nuclear Nonproliferation Treaty as a nonnuclear state.

Other items of contention in Russian-Ukrainian relations include: (1) the division of the Soviet Black Sea fleet between the two—both countries had agreed in principle by March 1992 on providing Ukraine with at least a minimal coastal defense force; (2) the political and territorial status of Crimea, which had been assigned by the U.S.S.R. to Ukraine after some two centuries of Russian rule in 1954; and (3) the division of the conventional military assets of the Soviet Army: due to Soviet military doctrine and practice, a disproportionate number of Soviet troops and armor was deployed in Ukraine. Consequently the tank forces stationed in Ukraine were larger than those of France and Germany combined (as well as of those deployed in Russia itself). The first two issues remained under negotiation as of mid-May 1992. At a Commonwealth of Independent States summit meeting in Tashkent on May 15, 1992, the post-Soviet states agreed to divide up the military assets of the U.S.S.R. as follows: Russia—54.1 percent; Ukraine—27.5 percent; Belarus—12 percent; with the remainder divided almost evenly between Armenia, Azerbaijan, Georgia and Moldova. At a commonwealth meeting of heads of government in Moscow on March 13, 1992, Ukraine acceded to pressures from Western creditors and agreed to assume joint responsibility with Russia and other commonwealth nations for the repayment of the Soviet foreign debt. (The Russian share is 61 percent; the Ukrainian, 16 percent.)

Impact of the Soviet Breakup
on U.S. Foreign Policy

How will the disappearance of the world's only other nuclear superpower affect the stability of the post-1945 order in East-West relations? What are the consequent challenges for the outside world, especially the United States, of this seismic shift in the weight and role of the Russian state? In thinking through this problem, it may prove helpful to consider two sets of relationships. The first set involves the ways in which the United States has been affected by, and reacted to, comparable instances of imperial disintegration in the nineteenth and twentieth centuries; and the second, the ways in which Soviet-American relations have been affected by the fact that the U.S.S.R. was a special kind of multinational state. The insights yielded by these two perspectives should help to frame the likely range of future conduct in relations between the United States and the post-Soviet successor-states.

On the first point, every breakdown of a major world empire from the Spanish to the British has had an important impact on American foreign policy. In many cases, the consequences of decolonization have caused considerable embarrassment for the United States in its relations with both the metropolitan power and the emerging independent states. Even during the period of alleged isolationism in American foreign relations, the United States was not able to remain unaffected by the breakup of major empires. This is certainly true today in the case of the breakup of the U.S.S.R., America's chief postwar rival.

On the second point, the impact of the multinational character of the Soviet state on U.S. foreign policy, the truth is that at no point in America's relationship with Soviet Russia, including the periods of nonrecognition and cold war, has this had a significant effect on Washington's policy toward the U.S.S.R. Throughout the 70-odd years of Soviet history, the United States, the public and officialdom alike, has held an image of the U.S.S.R. that is largely a reflection of how this country sees itself. The Soviet state, however detested, as well as Soviet society, was seen in essentially unitary terms, akin to the United States, with the differences between Ukraine and Russia held to be no greater than those between, say, New York and Texas.

During the period of nonrecognition, 1917–33, it was not the Soviet government's denial of self-determination for the nations within the empire that prevented official American dealings with Moscow. (In fact, the United States withheld recognition of the Baltic states' independence from Russia until 1922 in the hope that the restoration of constitutional government in Russia would thereby reestablish the continuity of the *imperial* Russian state.) Such obstacles to U.S. diplomatic recognition as Soviet repudiation of czarist debts, the Bolshevik seizure of American property, Soviet-inspired propaganda in the United States, and official Soviet atheism did seriously retard the normalization of Soviet-American relations in the 1920s. Yet once these problems had been resolved, or put aside (as they were in 1933), the repression of national self-determination within the U.S.S.R. would not serve to complicate greatly the course of relations between Moscow and Washington. American objections to the undemocratic nature of the Soviet system would remain a hindrance to any genuinely intimate set of relations with Moscow, but these criticisms were rooted in a general revulsion at the dictatorial character of the Soviet regime, and never—apart from the formal nonrecognition of Baltic annexation after 1940—at the specific subjugation of the nations, Russian and non-Russian, that composed the U.S.S.R. The Soviet dictatorship was seen as one over individuals, or even classes, but never in any politically important sense as a dictatorship over a multitude of nations. By contrast, the czarist system was viewed as "the prison house of nations," in language which Lenin helped make popular.

What is important for our analysis is not that Washington established its relations with the central Soviet authorities—which is standard diplomatic practice—but that it ignored the fact that the U.S.S.R., by virtue of being a multinational union, was a special kind of state. Throughout the early period of American recognition of the U.S.S.R., from 1933 on, the United States fully accepted as the foundation for Soviet-American relations the official Soviet view of the U.S.S.R., i.e., a single, legitimate state entity based on the voluntary union of its constituent national parts. (In the view of the United States, the three Baltic states, which were coerced into the U.S.S.R. seven years after U.S. recognition, fell into a different legal and political category than the other 12 Soviet republics, all of whom were also coerced into the union.)

Multinational Character of Soviet State

This tendency on the part of the United States to deal exclusively with the central Soviet authorities in Moscow, to the exclusion of the nations that made up the U.S.S.R., has been a consistent one in American foreign policy. That policy did not change even in recent times when the republics were progressively usurping the power of the center. Indeed, in certain respects, American policy was more respectful of Soviet interests than was the Soviet leadership itself: the Soviet constitution provided each of the 15 union republics with their own ministries of foreign affairs. Never, even during the depths of the cold war, did Washington entertain the possibility of establishing diplomatic relations with the republics, something which would have been entirely legal under the old Soviet constitution. At a minimum, Washington could have obtained a propaganda advantage by demonstrating, in the event of a Soviet rejection of such a relationship, the purely fictional character of the voluntary union that the U.S.S.R. claimed itself to be. At a maximum, the United States could have put itself in a much more favorable position to assess national developments within the U.S.S.R. and to react with intelligence and calculation to the nationalist forces that are now reconstituting the U.S.S.R. Thus, the entire course of Soviet-American relations, including the period before recognition in 1933, the early recognition period itself, certainly the years of wartime alliance from 1941 to 1945, and including the cold war itself, never found the United States making the multinational character of the Soviet state a significant consideration in its official Soviet policy. While the U.S. intelligence agencies did assist certain of the western populations of the U.S.S.R. in the late 1940s, primarily the western Ukrainians and the Baltic peoples as they resisted the reimposition of Stalinist rule, this never affected the formal assumptions of official U.S. policy toward the U.S.S.R. The problems the United States had with the U.S.S.R., it was held, could be negotiated or otherwise resolved with the central Soviet leadership; U.S. policies were directed toward affecting the U.S.S.R.'s leadership's calculus of costs and benefits in its American policy, not toward undermining its dictatorship at home and certainly not toward affecting the framework of relations governing the incorporation into the U.S.S.R. of its constituent nations.

Even the language of the "evil empire," as employed by President Ronald Reagan in the early 1980s, does not reflect any appreciation for the special, imperial character of the Soviet state. By evil empire, Reagan and those who shared his views meant simply that the Soviet Union was a bad though large state, imperial in its relations with the non-Soviet world (especially Eastern Europe), not that it was specifically imperialist in the manner in which it organized relations between the nations of the U.S.S.R. It was as if the U.S.S.R. were a unitary empire, after the fashion of the Founding Fathers' own vision of the great "American empire." Time and again in recent years, the U.S. government acted to strengthen Gorbachev's hand in confrontations with the forces of national separatism in the U.S.S.R. In essence, through diplomatic channels and public statements, the late Reagan and Bush Administrations made it clear that they were not prepared to recognize, de facto or de jure, national independence movements faster or in a more substantial way than was Gorbachev himself.

Until events forced its hand after the failure of the August 1991 coup, the U.S. government consistently chose not to respond affirmatively to the transformation of the Soviet Union. Even now, Washington does not seem to have an adequate concept for understanding the dynamic forces that are already forcing Western governments to make choices that their previous pro-Gorbachev policies were intended to avoid.

The United States now faces an increasing array of trying situations arising out of the former republics' desire for a greater international presence. These challenges will compel Washington to come to terms with the sovereign nationalisms of the countries of the former U.S.S.R. Indeed, the increasing activism of the newly independent former Soviet republics in the sphere of international politics is the cornerstone of an entirely new and still evolving pattern of international relationships emanating from the territory of the former U.S.S.R. They reflect what Harvard University scholar Roman Szporluk has called the process by which inter-ethnic relations have become genuinely international relations.

Distribution of Global Power

What *are* U.S. interests and how are they likely to be affected by the transformation of the U.S.S.R., whether the process be violent or peaceful and results in a stable reconfiguration of ties among the existing Soviet republics or a more chaotic set of political associations? The geopolitical interests at play have to be seen in light of the broader American stake in world politics. Apart from the question of survival as a nation, the primary American interest in international politics is that there be a plural and, if possible, stable distribution of global power. Contrary to widespread belief, the prosperity, security and political health of the United States do not depend on the reproduction of the American system worldwide, or even upon U.S. predominance in world affairs. It is sufficient for the protection and promotion of U.S. interests that such predominance be denied to any single state or group of states. Leaving aside the idealistic rhetoric, this was the reason for American intervention in the two world wars and for the policy of containment of the U.S.S.R. following 1947. The consequence of the global deployment of American power since 1945 has been the reestablishment of strong societies and political systems in Western Europe and Japan. This is the foundation for resistance to any prospective power who might seek hegemony over Eurasia, and thus the world. In fact, this well-anchored balance of power came into being long before the collapse of Soviet power in Europe in 1989.

In the final analysis, it will be the international, as opposed to the internal, conduct of states, including those of the former

U.S.S.R., that will prove decisive in framing American foreign policy choices on issues of vital interest to the United States. Change has occurred so rapidly in this area that the pace of change itself has become part of the problem.

The disintegration of the U.S.S.R. will continue to spawn an increasing number of new international relationships. At the same time, the collapse of the Soviet position in East Central Europe, which was the foundation of the country's entire global standing as a superpower, has diminished that area's importance for the United States. Developments in the region's political environment no longer have the significance that they had when the Soviet Union stood astride Central Europe as the world's second super-power. In the event of escalating violence in the former Soviet Union, the existence of a strong Western Europe, based on a powerful and unified Germany, and a dynamic East Asia, based on a forceful China and an economically (and potentially militarily) important Japan, provide effective "shock absorbers" against the spread of social, economic and political instability across former Soviet borders. There is very little that could happen in a geopolitical sense as a result of the disintegration of the U.S.S.R. that could affect vital U.S. security interests, as they have been traditionally conceived. William G. Hyland, former editor of *Foreign Affairs,* has noted in this respect that while the United States should try to assist a rapprochement between Eastern and Western Europe, "American interests in Eastern Europe have largely been satisfied with the collapse of the Communist regimes.... National tensions resulting from the disintegration of the U.S.S.R. do not have the potential of complicating relations with border areas of western China and the northern Middle East. The consequences of such tensions for America, even in the worst case, do not compare with the prospect of Soviet global hegemony that drove so much of U.S. foreign policy during the cold war."

This does not mean that the end of the U.S.S.R. will not have serious consequences, but they may just as easily be positive as negative. This is certainly true of the political forces represented by Russian President Yeltsin. Contrary to widespread consensus, Russian nationalism as expressed by Yeltsin is healthy in nature. Indeed, it is the first genuine expression of political nationalism in the history of Russia and is based, as Sovietologist Zbigniew Brzezinski has recognized, on the understanding that Russia can no longer afford to be an imperial state. A healthy nationalist concept, which Russia has always been denied, could actually provide the political basis for the acceptance of difficult economic reforms leading to a market-economy system. Such a market, if successful, could in the long run provide for a much more tightly integrated set of economic relationships between the nations that made up the former U.S.S.R. than was possible under the essentially mercantilist system of centralized economic planning that severely retarded the economic integration of the region. It is market forces that are the most effective agents of economic and eventually political integration, as evidenced most dramatically in Western Europe. Thus, there may not be a need for an "antidote" to Russian nationalism, as many have thought. A healthy Russian nationalism, as defined by a vigorous, nonimperial nationalist like Yeltsin, has to date been the best hope for containing ugly xenophobic and anti-Semitic forces, such as Pamyat—a militant Russian nationalist organization. Pamyat, which clothes itself in the mantle of Russian nationalism, has proved incapable of attracting the sympathy of Russian voters in a series of elections held since 1989.

The transforming of the U.S.S.R. into a group of independent states in loose association may in fact be the best hope for the peoples of the former U.S.S.R. as well as the outside world. Only on the basis of nationalist politics can a stable set of post-Soviet political systems be established. Whether nationalism, democracy and radical market reforms can be squared with each other is less certain. The international community, especially the United States, has little influence on a stable transition to a new political order within the existing U.S.S.R. Hyland has noted in this respect that "on most issues we are on the sidelines....It is really not up to the United States...to be the arbiter between Russia and, say, Ukraine or the five Central Asian nations, or to become the champion of the new commonwealth." Certainly, an unstable transformation of the U.S.S.R. would create considerable costs, mainly economic and social (refugees) for countries along the former Soviet borderlands, especially in Eastern Europe. Yet it is primarily Western Europe and Germany and, more broadly, members of the Conference on Security and Cooperation in Europe that are the appropriate vehicles for containing the damages which the shattering of the U.S.S.R. could cause abroad. On January 30, 1992, the CSCE admitted 10 of the former Soviet republics. (Russia had assumed the U.S.S.R.'s seat and Lithuania, Estonia and Latvia had been admitted in 1991. Only Georgia was frozen out.) In fact, given the smaller scale of their problems, their demonstrably greater commitment and progress toward democratic reform, and the degree of technical competence they have exhibited to date, Poland, Czechoslovakia and Hungary, in that order, might better be the focus of efforts to insulate the international system from the possible shocks of post-Soviet instability.

Major Foreign Aid Commitment

The outside world has in fact committed very substantial sums to the Soviet Union and the countries of the Commonwealth of Independent States. Between September 1990 and December 1991, about $80 billion in various forms of economic assistance had been pledged to the U.S.S.R. and its successor-states, according to data of the European Community. (This figure excludes debt relief and private humanitarian assistance.) Somewhat more than half of this sum is estimated to have been spent in significant measure to service the accumulated Soviet foreign debt. (Interestingly, Germany has provided $45 billion, or nearly 60 percent, of such aid; the United States, just 7 percent.) Furthermore, the United States and Germany, on behalf of the leading industrial countries, pledged an additional $24 billion in aid to Russia alone on April 1, 1992. (These figures are comparable to yearly expenditures on Lend-Lease aid to the U.S.S.R. in World War II and to Marshall Plan aid to Western Europe after 1947.)

Considerable differences exist concerning the efficacy of such assistance. Hyland has in fact stated that "most of the money will be wasted," while Brzezinski has cautioned that genuine recovery in the post-Soviet region will take almost a quarter century. On the other hand, Jeffrey D. Sachs, professor of economics at Harvard and an economic adviser to the Russian government, has argued forcefully that "reforms without aid would likely fail," and that Russian market reform "can succeed, now that it appears likely that the West will support Russia with the same vigor as Boris N. Yeltsin's government is pursuing economic reforms." The *Financial Times* of London has cautioned that Russian economic reform may succeed without Western aid, but that it may also fail with Western aid. These uncertainties suggest to the author that the United States should restrain its natural enthusiasm to engineer a solution to a problem that is only very partially susceptible to its influence.

Aggressive outside intervention is as likely to trigger a xenophobic backlash as it is to further the cause of reform. What the United States, and Americans, can do if they are to understand and respond helpfully to the current crisis in the post-Soviet region is, first, to revise their views of Russian nationalism and their preoccupation with any single political personality, such as Gorbachev or Yeltsin. They need to cast their vision of the area and the issues confronting the United States much more broadly. At a minimum, Americans should take care not to make their political and economic engagements with Russia and its neighbors a retardant to the positive disintegration that seems a prerequisite to the establishment of stable political relationships on the territory of the former U.S.S.R.

Nuclear Weapons Issue

There is another issue that arises from the political and nationalist convulsion of the U.S.S.R. and that far outweighs the question of the success or failure of political and economic reform: the question of the nuclear future of the nations that made up the U.S.S.R. Even during the height of the cold war, the logic of the nuclear age had imposed certain patterns of strategic collaboration on the U.S.S.R. and the United States, embracing arms control, confidence-building measures, strategic signalling, and the sharing of information necessary for the effective control of nuclear weapons. The prospect of the disintegration of a region bristling with more than 25,000 nuclear weapons is sure to reinforce the exclusively bilateral, Moscow-focused past U.S. policy. And for very good reasons: nuclear weapons are the only clear and present threat to vital American interests emanating from the territories of the U.S.S.R. The need to manage the nuclear relationship will continue to bind the U.S. government to those in the post-Soviet polities who control the instruments of mass destruction.

The Soviet general staff had already taken note of this problem before August 1991. In 1990 an arms race had begun within the U.S.S.R. itself, as contending nationalist forces resorted to raiding Soviet military arsenals in support of their own causes. Upward of 500,000 weapons, primarily small arms but including several surface-to-air missiles, tanks, helicopters and other armored vehicles, were stolen from the Soviet military. In early 1990, a Soviet military base in Azerbaijan containing nuclear weapons also came under attack. It is in this context that the then chief of general staff, Gen. Mikhail A. Moiseyev, declared in late September 1990 that the military had begun to move Soviet nuclear weapons based in certain non-Russian territories back to Russia.

As of mid-1992, Central Intelligence Agency (CIA) statements confirmed that there still exists tight central control over former Soviet nuclear weapons. But the question is, who is the center? Indeed, it is difficult to identify any agency of civilian control over the Soviet military's nuclear establishment outside of the person of President Yeltsin. In the aftermath of the August 1991 coup, which saw Gorbachev's codes for the release of nuclear weapons forcibly removed from his control, even this can no longer be taken for granted. In its annual review of Soviet foreign policy, the Soviet Foreign Ministry in early 1991 counted among the security threats facing the U.S.S.R. "the continuing risk of an accidental or unsanctioned use of arms. (This risk might increase in the event of internal disturbances in regions where strategic facilities are located.)"

After September 1991, Bush, Gorbachev and now Yeltsin acted with remarkable speed to reduce each country's nuclear forces by a set of unilateral but reciprocal steps that are aimed at eliminating short-range, tactical nuclear weapons, taking bomber and missile forces off their high states of alert, and reducing both countries' strategic nuclear forces well beyond the levels already agreed to in the strategic arms reduction treaty (Start), signed by the United States and the U.S.S.R. at the Moscow summit in July 1991. On June 16, 1992, both countries committed themselves to reduce their strategic nuclear arsenals from the current total of 22,500 to 6,500 by the turn of the century. Their actions have underscored both powers' determination to maintain effective central control over the Soviet nuclear arsenal.

Former CIA chief William H. Webster has raised a cardinal point that until late 1991 had hardly been examined in the political or academic communities in the United States, i.e., the relationship between domestic political order and nuclear weapons. The collapse of the U.S.S.R. challenges the unstated assumption of nuclear deterrence and arms control, namely, that the major nuclear powers are also stable states. Controlling nuclear weapons therefore must take into account the character of the political (and economic) systems of the nuclear states themselves. This represents a profound challenge to current thinking about nuclear arms control.

Some form of international oversight of the former Soviet nuclear weapons establishment seems necessary. A first step in this direction might be the rapid signing and ratification of the Nuclear Nonproliferation Treaty (NPT) of 1968 by the former republics, which are institutionally fully competent to do so. Such a measure would internationalize the pledges of Ukraine, Belarus and Kazakhstan to nuclear-free status. As part of such an arrangement, the scope of the International Atomic Energy Agency (IAEA) might be expanded to include supervision of existing nuclear-weapons facilities; alternatively, another UN verification body might be established. (Signatories to the NPT agree to follow IAEA safeguards, and the agency in turn has the right to inspect their peaceful nuclear facilities.) The expanded IAEA, among other responsibilities, could employ Soviet nuclear scientists as a guarantee against a danger that CIA chief Robert M. Gates warned of in December 1991: the diffusion of Soviet nuclear expertise to Third World countries in search of a nuclear capability. Conceivably, the Western nuclear powers might have to make some corresponding concessions, including international inspection, to make such a scheme highly acceptable. What is clear is that citizens of East and West need to confront, intellectually and politically, the necessity to reexamine approaches to deterrence and arms control that make security a hostage not merely to allegedly rational political actors, but also to potentially explosive and irrational political, social and economic forces.

U.S. Policy Considerations

The collapse of Soviet power has meant the end of the "Soviet threat," the energizing and unifying force behind American foreign policy throughout the postwar period. With that collapse has also ended any plausible challenge to the balance of power in Eurasia and thus the need to maintain large-scale American military forces in Europe and Asia. It was, after all, the threats posed to the Eurasian balance of power, first by Germany in 1917 and 1941 and later by the Soviet Union after 1945, that precipitated American involvement in two world wars and later the cold war. The disappearance of Soviet power thus completes the success of postwar American foreign policy: the reestablishment of West European countries and Japan as strong, stable, democratic governments has now been accompanied by the fragmentation of the Soviet Union into a set of polities—hopefully democratic but in any event likely to remain absorbed in their domestic affairs and in the management of their own set of post-Soviet international relations for decades to come. In this new geopolitical context there is no need for the United States to continue its postwar role as the chief pillar of the international balance of power. In the future, the United States can afford to reinforce and collaborate with international coalitions elsewhere; it need not embrace the hegemonial role that the vacuum of power in the post-1945 period encouraged it to assume. The multipolar world in international politics, prematurely forecast at the beginning of the 1970s, has now come to pass.

There are significant implications in such a new world order. One of them is certainly the relative increase in the geopolitical influence of an increasingly unified European Community, and within it Germany, on European, East European and world affairs. The unification of Germany in 1990 and the movement toward a single European economic market by 1993 make an increase in Europe's specific political weight inevitable. Moreover, in the final analysis, the ability of Europe, and in the first instance Germany, to anchor the East European states, and eventually the Soviet successor-states, in a strong European economic and political framework represents the strongest hope for long-term stability in that region. This is not to argue for, or predict, the complete withdrawal of U.S. military forces from Western Europe. Europeans East and West continue to see the United States as a stabilizing force in European affairs. The Pentagon has already begun to reduce its troop commitment in Europe from the more than 300,000 typical of the cold-war years toward 150,000, the Pentagon target for 1995. U.S. budgetary pressures, combined with eventual political changes in Germany, are likely to reduce those forces further. The challenge facing Americans in the near future is whether they are willing to field more than a purely symbolic force in post-cold-war Europe and, if not, are they prepared to accept the further diminution in political influence that such a refusal would entail?

U.S. Relationship with post-Soviet Commonwealth

In light of the disappearance of the U.S.S.R. and the formation of the Commonwealth of Independent States, the United States will have to develop a multilevel set of policies toward the post-Soviet region. Such policies will have to take into account the reality of the 11 sovereign republics in the commonwealth, in international as well as internal affairs, if it is to respond adequately to the prospects for post-Soviet reform and a maximally stable new world order.

There is, in addition, the question of whether the United States can have a constructive impact on such internal processes. The U.S. government has officially committed itself to promoting a stable transition to post-Soviet political and economic systems. In a major speech on December 12, 1991, at Princeton University, Secretary of State Baker outlined a concept for responding to what he termed the "historic" opportunities "to anchor Russia, Ukraine and other republics firmly in the Euro-Atlantic community and democratic commonwealth of nations." Arguing for a "collective engagement" policy "in support of freedom," Baker urged that, apart from immediate humanitarian needs, the United States and its allies need to (1) "help the Soviets destroy and control the military remnants of the cold war"; (2) help the commonwealth nations to "understand the ways of democracy to build political legitimacy out of the wreckage of totalitarianism"; and (3) "help free-market forces stimulate economic stabilization and recovery in the lands of the former Soviet Union." The secretary dramatically outlined the stakes as he saw them, stating that "a fall toward fascism or anarchy in the former Soviet Union will pull the West down, too. Yet, equally as important, a strong and steady pull by the West now can help them to gain their footing."

Until April 1992, however, U.S. assistance to the former Soviet lands had been but a fraction of the total Western assistance program. This led others, such as House majority leader Richard A. Gephardt (D-Mo.), to call for immediate accelerated humanitarian, especially medical, assistance; cooperation with Saudi Arabia in providing energy assistance to the area; and deferral of $9 billion in Russian interest payments to the West. In the longer term, Gephardt urged establishment of preferential trading status for the region, use of the American oil industry to develop commonwealth energy capacity, the export of computers and telecommunications products, as well as aid for U.S. business investment in Russia and other republics. Many others, such as Democratic presidential aspirant Arkansas Gov. Bill Clinton and Jeffrey Sachs, architect of the Polish economic "shock therapy," called for the establishment of an internationally guaranteed contingency fund, amounting to $5 billion to $6 billion, to help stabilize the value of the ruble.

By contrast, the international conference on aiding the former Soviet Union that was held in Washington, D.C., on January 22–23, 1992, was largely symbolic in character, with the U.S. Administration reluctant to commit significant resources to Russia and its neighbors in an election year in which nearly its entire political focus has been on domestic affairs. On April 1, 1992, in part in response to criticism from former President Richard M. Nixon and Governor Clinton that the Administration had been unduly slow in acting upon the challenge set forth by Secretary Baker, President Bush and Chancellor Helmut Kohl of Germany separately announced a $24 billion package of aid for the Russian Federation by the Group of Seven industrial nations. It included a fund to stabilize the ruble and help make it convertible with Western currencies; further rescheduling of $2.5 billion in Russian debt; loans from the IMF and World Bank; as well as commodity credits and direct humanitarian aid. A comparable sum was envisaged for the 10 other commonwealth countries. (The U.S. Congress at first resisted the program—the Freedom Support Act—barring more explicit commitments by the Bush Administration about the sources of such funds.) Only after the Bush-Yeltsin summit in mid-June 1992 did the Bush Administration make a strong political commitment in the Congress, and with the IMF, to accelerate passage of these aid measures, which by then had been supplemented by extension of most-favored-nation trading status, investment and taxation treaties, as well as dozens of other agreements on scientific cooperation, the environment, fishing rights, establishment of additional consulates, etc.

While the Administration's hesitancy to make good previous commitments to the commonwealth countries, partly as a result of parochial domestic considerations, is unfortunate, there are reasons to pause before engaging in an ambitious aid effort. There is first the enormous scale of the problem. Economist David Roche of Morgan Stanley has calculated that the scale of Western aid required if the Russian economic reform is not to be abandoned in midcourse is between $76 billion and $176 billion a year. This would provide direct aid for rebuilding infrastructure, revamping the energy sector, power stations, agriculture, training and welfare for the unemployed, and supplies of consumer goods. (Costs of cleaning the environment and the ruble stabilization fund are not included.) Secondly, there is so much that is not known about post-Soviet politics that caution would seem in order before embarking on what amounts to political-economic intervention in an unprecedented political upheaval. Actually, events have been pro-

Presidents George Bush and Mikhail Gorbachev at a press conference after signing Start agreement on July 31, 1991, in Moscow.

ceeding in a hopeful direction. In a first stage, 1991 witnessed a hasty but peaceful transition from union sovereignty to republican sovereignty, a process historically accompanied by large-scale violence. The Yeltsin government has since moved decisively on the path of market reform. Prior to that Yeltsin had already committed his country to free elections and the beginnings of meaningful constitutional government.

The outside world should be careful about the kind of role it tries to play. It is essential to keep in mind that any "solution" to the problems besetting the Russian nation be seen as a Russian solution and not as a foreign import (however much foreign advice is courted). As it brings its considerable moral and material weight to bear, the West can just as easily upset the process of mutual accommodation, especially by triggering a xenophobic backlash, as it can achieve its goals of sustaining reform. Throughout his trip to North America in mid-June 1992, Yeltsin gave voice to many of these issues. While welcoming foreign assistance, Yeltsin stated that Russia would not accept the "dictate" of foreign agencies that "did not know Russia or the Russian people"; that he was committed to reform apart from the question of assistance; and that it is private investment and not public assistance that is the key to addressing Russia's economic reconstruction.

Nuclear Arms Control Policy

The signature of Start, followed rapidly by further unilateral steps by both countries in September and October 1991, presented an opportunity to move quickly toward minimal levels of nuclear weapons on both sides. Start is the first agreement to codify the principle of reducing rather than simply ratifying existing levels of strategic nuclear weapons. Moreover, the treaty incorporates agreed principles for counting existing weapons systems, for reducing those systems, and for mandatory on-site verification.

In January 1992 Presidents Bush and Yeltsin went further in the area of long-range weapons: Bush proposed a 60 percent cut in strategic nuclear warheads, to some 4,700 ; Yeltsin in turn called for an 80 percent reduction in pre-Start force levels, to between 2,000 and 2,500 warheads on each side. On June 16, 1992, the two leaders announced their agreement to reduce to 3,000–3,500 warheads on each side by 2003. For the longer run, it should be noted that many experts, including former Secretary of Defense Robert S. McNamara, have been arguing that a policy of "minimal nuclear deterrence" could be established with as few as 500–1,000 nuclear weapons on each side. The collapse of the Soviet Union means that the political preconditions now exist in East-West relations, as well as in American politics, to review the minimal requirements for U.S. nuclear security.

Toward Multilateral Security

Signing and ratification of the Nuclear Nonproliferation Treaty by the former Soviet Union's republics would present an opportunity to build a more effective framework of multilateral security in the new world order. Russia is prepared for such a diplomatic move; the U.S.S.R.'s consistent support for U.S. policy in the UN to isolate and then defeat Saddam Hussein's Iraq—a long-time Soviet ally—affords convincing proof of this. The Persian Gulf war also demonstrated that the UN can be a cost-effective mechanism for maintaining the plural and stable distribution of international power that is the irreducible U.S. national interest in world politics. The question is whether Americans, politicians and the general public alike, will be willing to give up a degree of sovereignty and influence in specific situations in exchange for cultivating generally applicable principles of conflict resolution in international relations. For example, would the United States have accepted the subordination of its 1991 Persian Gulf military effort to a UN body, which would have meant a Chinese veto over operational strategy? In a related and more modest vein, are Americans willing to vote the appropriations for UN peacekeeping and military operations in which the United States may seldom play a central role (and for which the United States is currently $300 million in arrears)? In order to seize this opportunity, Americans will first have to confront, on the political as well as on the social level, the deeply rooted ambivalence in American society about the global role of the United States: In short, need compromise in international relations compromise American values at home?

From Cold War to Peace Dividend?

The United States in 1992 is confronting the consequences of success in its foreign policy. An enormous opportunity presents itself to the United States to initiate quickly and effectively a substantial reallocation of America's resources from the military to the civilian sphere and to rethink, without regressing into an illusory isolationism, the nature of its engagements with the wider world. The United States now faces the most unthreatening political-military environment in world politics since World War II. In William Hyland's words, "It is rare in history that a country can craft a wholly new foreign policy.... The United States now has that very opportunity."

Beneath the opportunity also lies an opportunity cost. The indices of social decay throughout the United States are so dramatic that a refusal to exploit the opportunity afforded by the end of the East-West competition will very likely serve to undermine the values of the United States that were presumably being defended on the front lines of the cold war. Sovietologists have pointed out that a handful of social indicators were enough to show the pathological crisis into which Soviet society had fallen: the drop in male life expectancy in the 1970s, the dramatic increase in infant mortality rates, and the quantum jump in female alcoholism. Consider the following facts:

- one of every four American children who has entered the first grade since the late 1980s lives below the poverty line;
- one half of all American high school students has used illegal drugs;
- black American males living in East Harlem have a lesser chance of living to age 40 than the average citizen of Bangladesh;
- life expectancy for the American black male population has been declining every year since 1985;
- the chances of an American urban black male between the ages of 15 and 24 being killed are higher than those of a GI in World War II (about one in thirty).

This is not to argue that the United States is destined to follow the Soviet path. The Soviet crisis was a general one, while social pathologies such as those mentioned above are confined to comparatively limited segments of American society. It does suggest, however, that America is losing control over too large a share of its patrimony.

Unlike the peoples of the former U.S.S.R., Americans—actually among the least heavily taxed of the advanced industrial democracies, and with a defense budget still pegged at cold-war levels ($280 billion to $290 billion)—can still choose their fate. This too is nothing less than an issue of vital national security. How Americans make that choice will say much about whether in winning their cold-war "victory" they have sacrificed the values over which the war was ostensibly fought, or whether America will enter the next century with its interests and values as secure as American cold-war policies intended them to be.

Talking It Over

A Note for Students and Discussion Groups

This issue of the HEADLINE SERIES, like its predecessors, is published for every serious reader, specialized or not, who takes an interest in the subject. Many of our readers will be in classrooms, seminars or community discussion groups. Particularly with them in mind, we present below some discussion questions—suggested as a starting point only—and references for further reading.

Discussion Questions

How do you evaluate Gorbachev's role in the disintegration of the U.S.S.R., especially his attempt to reconcile Soviet socialism with constitutional government?

What does the collapse of the U.S.S.R. signify for the way in which the United States defines its global foreign policy interests? Consider the following areas: the military budget, defense commitments, alliance relationships, nuclear-arms control.

What is the nature of the U.S. stake in post-Soviet reform? Consider the relationship between (a) economic reform, (b) political reform, and (c) international policies and conduct. What does this imply for the kinds of policies that the United States should pursue toward Russia and its post-Soviet neighbors?

How would you rate the prospects for stable political and economic development in the former Soviet territories? On what factors do you base your judgment?

Compare the national composition of the U.S.S.R. and its successor—the Commonwealth of Independent States—with that of the United States. Put special emphasis on Russia, Ukraine and Kazakhstan.

Discuss the possible impact of Islam on the future of the Commonwealth of Independent States and on Russia's relations with its Central Asian neighbors. What will be the involvement of other states, such as Turkey and Iran, in post-Soviet Central Asia?

READING LIST

Conquest, Robert, *The Harvest of Sorrow: Soviet Collectivization and the Terror-Famine*. New York, Oxford University Press, 1986. A chilling yet sober account of the terror-famine that struck the Ukraine in the 1930s.

Doder, Dusko, and Branson, Louise, *Gorbachev: Heretic in the Kremlin*. New York, Viking Penguin, 1990. A highly readable political biography of the Soviet leader.

Gaddis, John Lewis, *The Long Peace: Inquiries Into the History of the Cold War*. New York, Oxford University Press, 1989. An outstanding interpretation of the course of Soviet-American relations in the post-war period.

Gorbachev, Mikhail S., *Perestroika: New Thinking for Our Country and the World*. New York, Harper & Row, 1987. Gorbachev's explanation and defense of his attempt to save the Soviet system through far-reaching reform.

Lynch, Allen, *The Cold War Is Over—Again*. Boulder, Colo., Westview Press, 1992. Argues that 1989 saw the collapse not of the cold war but of the post-cold-war order in Europe, based on a divided Germany within a divided Europe. Contains much detail on themes raised in this HEADLINE SERIES.

Mandelbaum, Michael, ed., *The Rise of Nations in the Soviet Union: American Foreign Policy & the Disintegration of the USSR*. New York, Council on Foreign Relations Press, 1991. A collection of essays by five experts on the impact of the Soviet collapse on U.S. foreign policy.

Pipes, Richard, *The Formation of the Soviet Union: Communism and Nationalism 1917–1923*, rev. ed. Cambridge, Mass., Harvard University Press, 1964. The definitive work on the establishment of the multinational Soviet state.

Rothschild, Joseph, *Ethnopolitics: A Conceptual Framework*. New York, Columbia University Press, 1981. A major theoretical treatment of the problem of ethnicity in political life.

Shevardnadze, Eduard A., *The Future Belongs to Freedom*. New York, Free Press, 1991. The former Soviet foreign minister's defense of "new thinking" in Soviet foreign policy and of democracy at home.

Smith, Hedrick, *The New Russians*. New York, Random House, 1990. A very readable overview of Gorbachev's U.S.S.R.

Yeltsin, Boris, *Against the Grain*. New York, Summit Books, 1990. The Russian leader's political memoir.